RECORDS OF THE REGIMENTS OF THE SOUTH CAROLINA LINE
In The
REVOLUTIONARY WAR

Compiled by
ALEXANDER S. SALLEY

With an Index by
ALIDA MOE

CLEARFIELD

Excerpted from
*The South Carolina Historical
and Genealogical Magazine*
Volumes V-VII, 1904-1906

Reprinted with an Added Index
Genealogical Publishing Co., Inc.
Baltimore, 1977

By permission of
The South Carolina Historical Society
Charleston, South Carolina

Reprinted for
Clearfield Company, Inc. by
Genealogical Publishing Co., Inc.
Baltimore, Maryland
1991, 1992, 1995, 1997, 2003

Library of Congress Catalogue Card Number 77-76750
International Standard Book Number: 0-8063-0769-2

Copyright © 1977
Genealogical Publishing Co., Inc.
Baltimore, Maryland
All Rights Reserved

Made in the United States of America

RECORDS OF THE REGIMENTS OF THE SOUTH CAROLINA LINE, CONTINENTAL ESTABLISHMENT.

[In June, 1775, the 1st. Provincial Congress of South Carolina raised two regiments of foot and one of rangers for the defense of the Province in case the British Government should attempt coersive measures against the Province. In November, 1775, the 2d. Provincial Congress added a regiment of artillery, and in February, 1776, the same body added two regiments of rifles. By resolutions of the Continental Congress of June 18th. and July 24, 1676, and of the General Assembly of South Carolina of September 20, 1776, these six regiments were taken upon the Continental Establishment as South Carolina's quota, although they made a larger force than Congress demanded of South Carolina— larger than the relative population of the State warranted. The regiment of rangers was subsequently converted into infantry, and on February 11, 1780, the five infantry regiments were consolidated into three by order of Gen. Lincoln.* The records of these various regiments are scattered. Many of them are in the Record and Pension Office of the War Department; others are in the hands of libraries and historical societies; others are in private hands and still others have been irretrievably lost. Many of them are in possession of the South Carolina Historical Society and those are herewith given in chronological order.]

---

* See issue of this magazine for July, 1902, pp. 177-179.

[1.]

[INVENTORY OF CAPT. BLAKE'S COMPANY.[1]]

An Inventory of Arms, Accoutrements, and Cloathing Delivered Captain Blake's Company in 2 Regiment 1 January 1778

	Muskets	Bayonets	Pouches	Caps	Shirts	Coats	Waistcoats	Breeches	Stockings	Shoes	Blankets	No of Guns	Numbers property Destroyed	Stocks
119 per Steale														
120 per Norman														
Peter Upgreve Drum				1					1	1	1			
Josiah Kolb	1	1		1	11				1	11	1	146		
Robert Colman				1					1	1	1	153		
Wm McCullogh	1	1		1					1	1	1	148		
Daniel McIver	1	1		1					1	1	1	110	110	
Andrew Adams	1	1		1					· 1		1	132		
Thomas Burkett	1	1		1							1	136		
George Brynson	1	1		1					1	1	1	138		
Jacob Breyler	1	1		1					1		1	120		
5 Jacob Copland	1	1		1					1		1	118		
Timothy Downing	1	1		1					1	1	1	137		
James Freeman	1	1		1					1		1	134		
Peter Fagen	1	1		1					1	1	1	123		
John Fenwicke	1	1		1					1	1	1	124		
10 Richard Goodin	1	1		1					1	1	1	143		
Daniel Green	1	1		1					1	1	1	114		
William Hanson	1	1		1					1	1	1	145		
Samuel Horn	1	1		1					1	1	1	128		
Frederick Johnson	1	1		1					1	1	1	130		
15 John Jackson	1	1		1					1		1	115		
William Albert	1	1		1					1	1	1	117	Albert	
Wm Skipper Jones	1	1		1					1	1	1	133		
Anthony Hinds	1	1		1					1	1	1	126		
John Hinds				1					1		1	151		

[1] This inventory is incomplete. This and the records that follow it under Nos. 2, 3 and 4 are taken from a mutilated book containing, apparently, only records of Capt. Blake's company. The book has been much mutilated and even the records that have not been destroyed altogether have been much defaced, and memoranda of household matters have been jotted down among the records of the Revolutionary company.

[2.]
[AN AMENDED ORIGINAL ROLL.]

Roll of the Non Commissioned Officers, and Soldiers in Capt Blake's Company made 8th March 1778

Names	Rank	When made Non commissioned	Confin'd by	Crime	President	Day of sitting	sentence	Reduced	Pardoned or part remitted	Discharged	Deserted	Dead	Observations
Wm Brown	sergeant												
Jonah Kolb	sergeant												
Robt Colman	sergeant	1st Novr 77											
Wm McCullogh	Corporal										Discharged		
Danl McIver	Corporal										Discharged		
Peter Ugrove	Drummer										Discharged		Promoted
Andrew Adams	Private										Discharged		
Thos Burkett	Private										Discharged		
Geo Brynson	Private		Lt Colonel	Desertion	Capt Lesesne	12th Feb78	99 Lashes		Picketting	Discharged			
Jacob Breyser	Private										Discharged		
J Copland	Private										Do		
Timy Downing	Private										Discharged		
Jas Freeman	Private											29 Nov 78	Transfered
Peter Flaten	Private												
Jno Frowerke	Private												
Kird Goodin	Private												
Danl Green	Private												

Names	Rank	When made Non Commissioned officers	Confin'd by	Crime	President	Day of Sitting	Sentence	Reduc'd	Pardoned or part remitted	Discharg'd	Deserted	Dead	Observations
Wm Hanson	Corporal		Lt Cole	beating & abusing Serjt Simpson	Capt Baker	18 Decr 78	Reduced						Exchanged 20 Jany 79
Neal Horn										Discharged			
Fredk Jackson										Do			
Jno Jackson										Do			
Wm Jenkins										Do			
Wm P Jones										Do			
A Hinds										Discharged			
Jno Hinds										Do			
G Knolton										Discharged			
Thos Lampley			Warley Lt Colonel	Neglect of Duty Desertion	C Charnock Cole Henderson	21st Febr	Death		Pardoned	de		Dead	Transfered.
Jno Lyons													
Jno LeFevre													
Rode Moody													
H Mc Lean													
Wm Normand													
Jas Oliver										Discharged			
F Pickring										Do			
Benj Reeves													
Jno Steele										Discharged			Transfered
Jhon Shedy													
Thos Smith													
Alexr Stuart													
Wm Sims													
Thos Shora										Discharged			
Siega Strachan										Do			
Wm Tapier										Do			
Isaac Wilson													
Jno Whitsett													
Joe Whitaker													
Rowland Thomas												Dead	
James Oakes											Deserted		
Ridd Yearby											Deserted		
Wm Harper													
James O'Neal	Enlisted		Lt Colonel 78	Desertion	Capt Lesesne	12th Feb78	99 Lashes	9 Febr 79	Picketting				Transfered to 5th Regt
Arvil Upgrove	Corporal	31 Augt											Promoted 20 Jany 79
Lake Kindall	Corporal												Promoted 20 Jany 79
J Jordan Camsbee													
Henry Savage													
Moses Brunk													

[3.]

[ROLL OF THE COLONEL'S COMPANY, SECOND REGIMENT.]

Inventory of Arms &c Cloathing &c Delivered to the Colonel's Company 28 June & 7 September 1778[2]

Jn⁰ Roberts			
Alex^r Stuart	Astlow	1	⎫
Daniel Green	Brown	1	⎪
Wm Hanson	Markey	1	⎪
Wm Albert	Green	1	⎬ Rec^d 15 April 1779
Andrew Adams	Collins	1	⎪
Moses Bruce	Connell	1	⎪
Jn⁰ Caves	Williams	1	⎪
Jn⁰ Caddy	Batheny	1	⎪
Tim Downing	Swall	1	⎭
Peter Fagen			
Jn⁰ Fenwicke	Wilkins	1	⎫
Richd Goodwin	Serj Bonett	1	⎪
Saml Horn	Parker	1	⎪
Jn⁰ Lyons	Gibson	1	⎪
Mc Lean	Staple	1	⎬ Diff^t Times
Wm Norman	Fenicke	1	⎪
Ja^s Oakes	Wailes	1	⎪
Benj Reeves	Morgan	1	⎪
Jn⁰ Shudy	Hagarthy	1	⎭
Thos Shoars			
Stepⁿ Strecham	Webster	1	⎫
Wm Tapper	Mace	1	⎪
Arch^d Upgrove	Clyatt	1	⎬ at Sheldon
Jn⁰ Whitset	Taylor	1	⎪
Ge⁰ Brynson	Richson	1	⎭
Fred^k Smith	Horne	1	
Wm Cook 1.			
Lamb			

[2] These dates have been stricken out, whether originally or by some mischievous hand is debatable. Although characterized as an inventory in the heading this paper was evidently never finished, but was converted into a list of the Colonel's Company with the names added of certain men subsequently recruited.

[4.]

[RECEIPTS FOR ARMS.]

Received 1 July 78 of Lieut Baker 3 Reg^t Muskets, 3 Bayonets, & one Pouch belonging to his Company [3]
Received 3 July of Lieut Baker 6 Muskets, 6 Bayonets, & 3 Pouches William Fletcher Q^r Mast^s Sety

Rec^d 11 Augt 78 of Lt Baker 12 Muskets 12 Bayonets 3 Pouches belonging to men discharged from his Comp^y
        Daniel Simpson Sarj^t

---

[3] This receipt was scratched over.

RECORDS OF THE REGIMENTS OF THE SOUTH CAROLINA LINE, CONTINENTAL ESTABLISHMENT.

[5.]

[ORDERS FOR THE 3D. REGIMENT.]

New Barrack 1 July 1778

General Orders by } Parole *Fayette*.
General Moultrie

Regimental Orders by }
L^t. Colonel Mayson

That a Regimental Court Martial do sit immediately, where the President may appoint, for the trial of such Prisoners as may be brought before them.

Lieut Isaac Crouther President

Lieuts { Fitzpatrick, DeSaussure } Members
       { R Jones, Robison }

That all Officers & men off duty do attend divine Service at 10 OClock to morrow morning.—

That the Captains, or Officers having Charge of Companies, do deliver to the Commanding Officer a Duplicate of their Muster Rolls by the 8th, Instant.—

Capt. Uriah Goodwyn being taken sick Capt D. Hopkins Officer of the day to Day

Capt D. Hopkins of the Day

Lieut^s. { Crouther }
         { Robison } for Guard } Officers to morrow—
         { Newsom   }

☞ James Stuart of Capt Towles Company deserted 30 June 1778

2^d July 1778

General Orders by }
General Moultrie }

Parole Elbert

[6.]

[A LETTER OF CAPT. RICHARD MASON.[4]]

Charles Town 10th. March 1779

This will be handed you by Capt. Bremar Who is Order'd to Camp to Muster the Regts. of Our State[5] Who I doubt not Will Receive Every Civility in yr. Power When amongst yr. Corps as he is a Stranger to them in General.—Yesterday Mentor Acquainted me you had Lost Your favourite Grey Gelding—I have for Got both his Name And Wether or Know he was branded and What brand if you Could Send me his Marks and brands As I Expect to Go a Recruiting I may perhaps met With him in my Travels—Your Smallest Sow has been almost killed by some of the Soldiers the Other is Now With Piggs if you think proper I Will Either take the Sows at a Reasonable Rate and pay you or yr. Order or Keep the Sows for you allowing a Reasonable price for any Pig I may kill from them—Your Answer Will Greatly Oblige yr Most

Hble Servt.—

Richard Mason

[7.]

[WILLIAM KENNEDY'S PASS.]

The bearer William Kennedy formerly lived in Georgia but fled over to this State with his Wife & family he lives near the general hospital at Mr. Browns place he wants to look for a Mare & Colt upon the Sandhills—he is esteemed an

---

[4] This was among the papers left by Major Isaac Harleston and must have been addressed to him. [5] Francis Bremar, Deputy Muster Master, certified to the muster roll of Capt. R. B. Roberts's company of the regiment of artillery of the South Carolina Line, Continental Establishment at Purrysburgh, March 19, 1779. (See Gibbes's *Documentary History of the American Revolution*, 1776-1782, pp. 109-110.).

honest young Man if it is thought prudent to let him pass—
John Smith

   7th April 1779

[8.]
[GUARD AND PICKETS AT PURRYSBURGH.]
A report of the Guards & piquets in & near Purisburgh
March 16/17 1779
Parole Ulysses Count[ns].. Union }
Unity }

Prisoners Names	Regiments	Companys	Confin'd by	N⁰ of nights	Crimes
Thomas Medcalf	.	.	Gen[l]. Rutherford		Enemy to States
George Rardall	... ...	... ...	Maj[r]: Wise	..	Treason & Perjury
John Crawford	3[d]. S⁰ Carolina	Capt[n] Goodwin	Maj[r]: Wise		Desertion
Thomas Crawford	6th. S⁰ Carolina	.	L[t] C[l]. Henderson	..	D⁰
William Brooner	6 S⁰ Carolina		L[t] Lytle		Sleeping on Post
James Sims	. .	. .	. . . .	... ...	{ For endeavouring to make the soldiers discontented with Constitution & attempting to induce them to desert

Main Guard
Capt[ns]. Sub[ns]. Serj[ts]. Corp[ls]. D: & fifes. priv[ts]. Centries by Day. d⁰ by night
1 1 2 2 2 36 5 8

Zubly's
Capt[ns]. Sub[ns]. Serj[ts]. Corp[ls]. D: & fifes. priv[ts]. Centries by day. d⁰ by night
1 1 3 2 — 45 6 13

Swamp
Sub[ns]. Serj[ts]. Corp[ls]. D: & fifes. priv[ts]. Centries by Day. d⁰ by night
1 1 1 — 18 4 5

Road piquet
Sub[ns]. Serj[ts]. Corp[ls]. D: & fifes. priv[ts]. Centries by day. d⁰ by night
1 1 1 — 18   5

Galleys
Serj[ts]. Corp[ls]. D: & fifes. priv[ts]. Centries by night
1 1 — 12 3

Bullocks
Serj[ts]. Corp[ls]. priv[ts]. Centries by night
1 1 9 2

Kailes
Serj[ts]. Corp[ls]. priv[ts]. Centries by night
1 1 9 2

River Guard
Serj[ts]. Corp[ls]. priv[ts]. Centries by night. d⁰ by day⁵

Generals Guard
Sub[ns]. Serj[ts]. Corp[ls]. priv[ts]. Centries by day. d⁰ by night
1 1 1 18 3 6

Grand Rounds visited from One to 5 oClock
Thomas Pinckney
Major 1st. Reg[t]. S. C.
F. O. D.

⁵This column scratched out on original.

[RETURN OF THE 1ST. REGIMENT.]

Return of the First Regiment of South Carolina, of Foot, Commanded by Colonel Charles Cotesworth Pinckney.

Companies	Officers present fit for duty														Non Commission'd					Rank & File					Wanting to Complete			Alterations since last return							
	Field			Commission'd				Staff					Serj't Major	Quartermaster Serj't	Drum Major	Fife Major	Serjeants	Drum'rs & fifers	Present fit for duty	Sick present	Sick Absent	On Command	On Furlough	Total	Serjeants	Drum'rs & fifers	Rank and File dead	Discharged	Deserted	Sent to the Corps of Invalids	Promoted	Serjeants	Drum'rs & fifers	Rank & file	When join'd
	Colonel	Lieut Colonel	Major	Captains	First Lieutenants	Second Lieut's	Chaplain	Adjutant	Pay Master	Quarter Master	Surgeon	Mates																							
Field and Staff Officers	1	1	1					1	1	1	1	2	1	1	1	1																			
Grenadiers				1	1													2	2	14	4		2		20			55		1						
Light Infantry				1	1	1												2	1	17	2	1			20		1	55								
Captain Hyrne					1													2	1	14	3	2	1		20		1	55		8						
Captain Vanderhorst				1	1	1												2	2	19	6				27			48		2						
Captain Drayton				1	1	1												2	1	16	3	1			20		1	55		1						
Captain Turner				1	1													3	2	15	2	1	1	1	18	1	0	57		2						
Captain Theus																		2	1	15	2	2			18	1	1	57		2						
Captain Elliott				1	1	1												2	1	14	1	1			19			56		2						
Captain Linning				1		1												3	2	15	2			2	19			55		2						
Captain Gadsden				1														3	2	17	2		1		20					3						
Totals	1	1	1	6	7	4		1	1	1	1	2	1	1	1	1		20	16	156	7	25	13	1	202	4	2	548				1				

Sick present .... | 1 | | | | | | | | | | | | | | | | | | | | | | | | | | | | | | | | | | | |
Vacant .... | | | | | | 4 | | | | | | | | | | | | | | | | | | | | | | | | | | | | | | |

Absent Officers Names	Places where	Reasons for And time of Absence
Cap't Hyrne	Head Quarters	Adjutant General
Captain Turner	Northward	Aid de Camp to General Howe
Lieut Levachar	Cha's Town	Sick
1'st L't Frazer	Georgia	Prisoner of War

22 | 1 Captain Gadsden on Command
    | 1 Lieut Skrvrung ...... ditto
    | 2 Serj'ts on Command, Viz't Dodd to Gen'l Bulls &
    | J'no Brown with Cap't Gadsden
    | 13 privates on Command with Cap't Gadsden
    | 2 Serjeants sick in Charles Town
    | 2 Serjeants Absent with Leave
    | 1 Fife Major Sick in Charles Town
    | 12 privates sick in ditto
    | 2 Drummers sick in Gen'l Hospital
    | 11 privates sick in ....ditto.
    | 2 privates sick in flying hospital

N. B: Charles Mc Neil Gunner of Fort Moultrie and 3 privates prisoners of War are not Included in the above return—

Thomas Pinckney
Major 1'st Reg't S. C.

Endorsed: May 1'st- 1779
Monthly return
of First regim't
May 1'st .. 1779

[10.]

[REPORT OF THE 1ST. REGIMENT.]

A Report of the 1st: Rigt of South Carolina
May 5th: 1779.

	Sarjt-	Corpl	privat
Presant in Camp...............	3	3	28
Sick Left at Capt. Hamton	1	1	6
Totol	4=	4=	34

Sarjt Gruver Corpril Cochrin Mikel Nash Rolin Williams Robert Hines Joseph Butler Bunker Thring Jo^n- Cosang John Vanderhorst Capt

[11.]

[REPORT OF A COURTMARTIAL.]

Addressed: Maj^r. Harleston
6th So Carolina
Reg^t ———

Agreeable to Order of Maj^r. Harlestons June 5th 79 a Regimental Cortmartial sat for the tryal of Joseph Marques & Ezekiel Adams———

President Capt. Doggett
Capt Warley } members } Lieu^t. Pollard

Joseph Marques of Capt Doggett Comp^y. is Charg^d. with absence without leave the prisoner Confeses guilty and sais he was drunck and was persuaded away and that he intended to Return amediately, the Cort Considering his former Carrecter and the first offence is of the oppinion he ought to be acquited—

Ezekiel Adams of Capt Buchannans Comp^y. Charged with being absent at tattoo and abuseing his wife he confesses being absent but denies abuseing his wife, he sais he was only in play with her the Cort Considering the Prisoners Charge and defence Sentence him to Receive Thirty five Lashes—

R^d,, Doggett Presidnt
Capt Boyes

[12.]

[COURTMARTIAL FINDINGS.]

Regimental Orders by Major Harleston June 7 1779
a Court Martial to set for the trial of Joseph Marquise & Ezekiel adams with such Other prisoners as shall be brought before the Court

Capt Warley President—
Captⁿ Boyes Members Lt Pollard.

Joseph Marquise brought before the court charg^d with Absenting himselfe without leve, pleads Guilty—but says in his defence that he was drunk and pursuaded away by Stewart, otherwise he never Should absented himselfe, and begs the Mercy of the Court the Court are of Opinion that he shall Receive 100 Lashes On his bare back with Switches.

I approve
I Harleston
Major

Ezekiel Adams brought before the court charg with being drunk, and absent at tattoo beating, pleads guilty of being absent but denies drunkenness, The prisoner says in his defence that he was up the night before on Guard, and that he was Sleepy and layd himselfe down, went fast asleep and

never heard tattoo beat. The Court are of Opinion that he shall Receive 50 Lashes On his bare Back with cat nine tales
I approve
I Harleston Major

Serjeant Johnston of Captain Taylors company brought before the court charg^d with disobedience of Orders and Neglect of duty, pleads not guilty, Serjeant Major being being examined. Says that he warnd Sarj^t Johnston last nigh and this morning for guard. when the Troop Beat and the men paraded, Sarj^t Johnston did not attend on the Regimental parade· I cauld for him Several times after. and he would not come, at the grand parade when Sarj^t Johnston was for that duty which he did not attend, I Also Ordered another in his place and confin'd him for the Neglect, The prisoner says in his defence that he was at Breckfast when he was cauld for and made Answer that he was acomming but the Guard march^d of before he got there The court are of Opinion that he is Guilty, and Shall be Reduced to a private Centinal.
I approve I Harleston Major

Oliver McHaffey brought before the court charg^d with absence without leve pleads not guilty, L^t pollard evidence against the prisoner. Says that the prisoner left the Reg^t about the 15th of last month, which he never seen him untill yesterday, The prisoner says in his defence that he was pursuaded away by One of the 3^d Reg^t, being a young soldier and did not know the Consequence of going away. he begs the court will forgive hime, this time for he should never do the like again. The Court Are of Opinion that he is guilty and Shall receive 60 Lashes with Cate nine tales but Recommend him to Mercy being a young Soldier
I approve but remit 20 Lashes   Captain George Warley
 I Harleston   President
  Major 6th Reg^t.

RECORDS OF THE REGIMENTS OF THE SOUTH CAROLINA LINE, CONTINENTAL ESTABLISHMENT.

[13.]

[PAY ROLL OF THE 3D. REGT., AUG., SEPT. AND OCT., 1779.[6]]

Pay Roll of Capt Felix Warley's Company for August, Sept^r.. & October 1779

Rank	Names	Pay & Subsistence in Dollars	Receipt
Capt	Felix Warley	929.30	Felix Warley
1st Lieut	Lewis DeSaussure	333.20	D. DeSaussure Adm^r
Serg Maj	Isaac Vaughan	54.60	Isaac Vaughan
Q. M. Sergt	Robert Johnston	54.60	Robt Johnston
Fife Maj	William Haslam	54.60	Wm Haslam
Arm.	Frederick Ward	54.60	
Serg	Daniel Norwood	75.	
"	Adam Martin	54.60	Adam Martin
"	Robert Bird	54.60	Robert Byrd
Corp	Robert Dewley	46.60	Robert ✕ Dewley
"	William Pullam	46.60	Wm Pullam
Drum	Tartle McCloud	29.	
Fife	John Whaley	46.60	John Whaly
Private 1.	William Anderson	44.60	Wm ✕ Anderson
2	Isaac Andersor	44.60	Isaac ✕ Anderson
3	John Barnett	44.60	
4	James Banks	"	James ✕ Banks
5	William Bean	"	Wm ✕ Bean
6	James Bean	"	James ✕ Bean
7	James Black	"	James ✕ Black

[6] This pay-roll is in the library of Yale University, and a certified copy thereof was made several years ago by Lucetta E. Fenner for Mrs. Winborn Wallace Lawton, of Charleston, S. C., who has kindly permitted it to be copied and printed here. The first general return of this regiment was published in the issue of this magazine for July, 1901.

RECORDS OF THE SOUTH CAROLINA LINE

8	Joseph Brooks	"	Joseph X Brooks
9	Isaac Boon	"	Isaac X Boon
10	Charles Berry	"	
11	Benjamin Binam	"	Ben Bynum
12	Nathaniel Connors		
13	Elisha Chavers		Elisha X Chavers
14	George Cates		George X Cates
15	Charles Devors		Charles Devis

carried forward.   Capt Felix Warleys Comp: Cont^d..

Rank	Names	Pay & Sub^s. in Dolls	Receipt

Private brot forward

16	Maurice Fowler	44.60	Maurice Fowler
	John Gicken		
	Robert Gibson		Robert Gibson
	John Gillon		John Gillen
	Thomas Horner		Thos Horner
	Michael Houselighter	44.60	Michael X Houselighter
	Wm Hardick		Wm X Hardick
	John Jackson		John X Jackson
	Ezael John		Ezael X John
25	Joseph Joyner	44.60X	Joseph X Joyner
	John King	33.20	
	James Kirkpatrick	44.60	James Kirkpatrick
	Thadius Lassiter	32.60X	
	James McElwee	44.60	James McElwee
	John Martin		John X Martin
	Hugh McCullough		Hugh X McCollough
	Philip Moore		Philip X Moore
	Edward McKoy	33.30	Edward X McKoy
	James Read	44.60	James X Read
	William Stewart		William X Stewart
	Charles Steele		Charles X Steele
	Peter Temples		Peter X Temples
	William Upshaw		William Upshaw
	Ezekiel Wilson		Ezekiel X Wilson
	Edward Wells		Edward Wells
41	Joseph Windsor	44.60	Joseph X Windsor

3628.10

Pay Roll of Capt David Hopkins Comp^y.. for Augt Sep^t & October 1779.

Rank	Names	Pay & Sub. in doll^s. —90th	Receipts
Capt.	David Hopkins	626.	D. Hopkins
1st Lieut	Luke Mayson	333.20	Luke Mayson
Ser-Jants	John McGee	55	Jno McGee
	John Humphreys	55	John Humphreys
Corp.	Isaac Haddocks	46.82	Isaac × Haddocks
	Demsey Thomas	46.82	Demsey × Thomas
drum^r..	Joseph Roy	46.82	Joseph × Roy
Priv^ts.. 1.	Saml. Goar	33.20	
	John Hunter	44.80	John × Hunter
	Robt Kennady	44.80	Robt × Kenaday
	Ezekiel Camble	44.80	Ezekial Camble
	Henry Gousmald		
	John Loveman		John × Lovemon
	James Gough		James × Gough
	Findlay McCaseel		Finlay McCaskill
	James Cantley		James Cantley
	Joel Stow		
	John Bunch		John × Bunch
	Thos Wicham		Thos × Wicham
	Saml. Sutton		Samuel Sutton
	John Pearce		John × Pearce
	James White		James × White
	John Ragsden		John × Ragsden
	George Hope		George × Hope
	John Boothe		John × Booth
	Saml. Oliver		Saml.. Oliver
	Jonathan Lipencott		Jonathan Lipencott
	John Inlow		John × Inlow
	Thos. Harris		Thomas × Harris
23	Peter McGraw		Peter × McGraw

Carr^d Forw^d..

Capt David Hopkins Comp^y. Cont^d..

Rank	Names	Pay. &c	Receipts
Privates Brot Fow^ds.			
24	Fred Hackles		
	John Cample		
	Mathew Morrow		Mathew × Morrow
	Fred Sellers		Fred × Sellers
	Jacob Temples		Jacob Temples

RECORDS OF THE SOUTH CAROLINA LINE

	John White		
	Esau Smith		
	Charles Quail		Charles × Quail
32	John Hellary		John × Hellary

Capt John C. Smiths Pay Roll for Augt. Septr and October 1779.

Rank		Names	pay and subsist- in dollars 90th	Receipts
Capt.		John C Smith	626	Jno. C. Smith
1 Lieu^t.		Joel Hardaway	333.20	J. Hardaway
Serjt$_s$ {		Philip Pearce	55	
		Charles Mulherin	55.	Chas. Mulherin
Corp. {		Thomas Morris	46.82	Thos Morris
		Jos. Mills	46.82	
drum^r.		John Peterkin	46.82	John Peterkin
Priv.	1	Bland Blackley	46.82	Blan Blakley
	2	Jacob Brazil	44.80	Jacob × Brazell
	3	Benjn Carter	44.80	Benj. × Carter
		John Bone	44.80	John × Bone
		Geo Carter		Geo × Carter
		Saml. Campbell		Saml× Campbell
		Will. Crane		
		Tho. Dean		thomas deen
		John Dean		John Deen
		Easum Franklin		Easum × Franklin
	11	John Fulmer		John × Fulmer

Capt.. John C Smiths Company Continued

Rank	Names	pay &c	Receipts
Priv^t..	Brot Forward		
12.	Jesse Farrar	44.8	Jesse × Farrar
	John Fleming		John × Fleming
	Ashford Gore		Ash × Gore
	James Galaspie		James × Galaspie
	Henry Hogwood		
	Thos. Herindine		Thos × Herindine
	Carter Hamlet		Carter Hamlett
	Rich^d. Jones		Rich^d.. × Jones
	Henry Keller		Henry × Keller
	John Mar .. Matts		John M × Matts
	John Millar		John Miller
	Benjamin Paybody		

18 RECORDS OF THE SOUTH CAROLINA LINE

	Willm. Peoples		Wm × Peoples
	John Shannon		John Shannon
	Thomas Taylor		
	Thos. True		Thos × True
	Jacob Watson		Jacob × Watson
	Will Wright		Wm × Wright
	Rob. Willson		Robt. × Willson
	Jonathan White		
33	Thomas Anderson		
	Thomas Burns		Thomas Burns
	John Haze		John × Haze
	James Haze	44.80	James × Haze
	James Tinsley	3.70×	
	Abram Evans	3.70×	
39	Joseph Rhodes	3.70×	
		─────	
		2825.56	

Captn. Jos. Warleys Pay Roll for Augt Sept^r & October 1779.

Rank		Names	Pay & subsis^n. dolls. 90	Receipts
Capt.		Joseph Warley	626	Joseph Warley
2 Lieut		Robert C. Baillie	240.30	
Serj^ts..	{	Wm Carless	54.60	Wm Carloss
		Wm Taylor	54.60	Wm Taylor
Corp	{	Michael Finney	46.60	Michael × Finney
		James Scott	46.60	
		Isaac Gassett	46.60	Isaac × Gassett
drum^r.		Duncan M^cpherson	46.60	Duncan × M^cpherson
Fifer		Will Henson	44.60	Wm × Henson
Priv^s.	1	John Owens	44.60	John × Owens
		John Steel	44.60	John × Steel
		John Lee		John × Lee
		Saml Kelley		Saml × Kelly
		John Finney		John × Finney
		James Ashbury		James ×. Ashbury
		Squire Madcap		Squire × Madcap
		John Lawrence		John × Laurance
		Moses Downer		
	10	Ahas Rogers		Ahas Rogers
		Robt Campbell		Robert ×. Camble
		Atheal Perkins		Atheal × Purkins
		John Pennington		John × Pennington
		Edwd.. Petty		Edwd.. × Petty

RECORDS OF THE SOUTH CAROLINA LINE 19

	Names	Pay	Receipts
	John Sadler		John ✕ Sadler
	Geo Scott		George Scott
	Alex^r. McGuire		
	Geo. Myers		Geo ✕ Myers
	Chris^r Andy		Christ^r: ✕ Andy
	John Smith		John ✕ Smith
21	John Sibley	44.80	John Sibley
22	William Sibley		William Sibley
23	James Finney		James finney

Capt Jos. Warleys Company contin^d..

Rank Pri.	Names	Pay &c	Receipts
	brot.. Forw^{rds}=		
24	Will Jones	44.60	Wm ✕ Jones
	Jos. Haynes	44.60	Joseph Haynes
	Charles McCormack		Charles ✕ McCormack
	Will Notcher		Wm ✕ Notcher
	Dennis McCarty		Dennis McCarty
	Wm Crimm		Wm ✕ Crim
	Edward Broadaway		
	Cornelius Rose		
	Burrel Wittenton		
	Isaac Wittenton		Isaac ✕ Wittenton
	Elijah Jones		
	Rich^d. Ward		Richard ✕ Ward
	Reason Jinkens		
37	Richd Norwood		
38	Will. Brown		Wm Brown.

Capt.. Uriah Goodwins Pay Roll for Augt. Sept^r.. & Oct^r.. 1779.

Rank		Names	Pay & subs. in dolls. 90	Receipts
Capt..		Uriah Goodwin	626	U Goodwin
1 Lieut		Aaron Smith	333.20	Aaron Smith
2 Lieut		William Love	333.20	W Love
Ser'jt	⎰	Johnston Elkins	55	Johnson Elkins
	⎱	William Jones	61.40	Wm Jones
		William Chapman	55.	William Chapman
Corp.	⎰	Benjamin Lewis	46.60	Benjn ✕ Lewis
	⎱	Arthur McGraw	46.60	Arthur ✕ McGraw
Fife		John Goodwyn	46.82	John ✕ Goodwyn
Privt	1	John Clarke	44.80	John Clark
	2	John Tann	44.80	John ✕ Tann
		carr^d Fow^d-		

Capt. Uriah Goodwyn's Company cont^d..

Rank Priv^t.	Names Amt brot. forw^d..	Pay &c	Receipts
3	Michael Matts		Michael × Mats
	Jacob Salters		Jacob × Salters
	Joshua Ammonds		Joshua × Amonds
	Benjamin Gordon		Benjn.. × Gordon
	Edward Falkner		
	John Archart		John Archart
	John Haskins		John hasskin
	Jacob Meaddows		Jaob × Meaddows
	John McCafferty		John × McCafferty
	William Skeen		Wm × Skean
	John McCune		John × McCune
	Wilkins Harper		Wilkins Harper
	David Myrtle		
	James Johnston		James × Johnston
	Croker Crowley		
	Thomas Barker		Thos. Barker
	Alexander McCartey		
20	James Willson		
21	William Chapman		William Chapman
	Elijah McGuire		Elijah Mguire
	James Ginkins		James × Ginkins
	Joseph Spencer		Joseph × Spencer
25	Jessey Smith		Jesse Smith

Capt. Uriah Goodwyn's Company Cont^d..

Rank Priv^t..	Names	Pay &c	Receipts
26.	Hardy Stewart	44.80	Hardy × Stewart
27.	James Nipper	91.70	
	John Bowen		John × Bowen
	Mathew Declendenese	44.80	Mathew × Declandenease
	Isaac Veach	44.80	Isaac × Veach
	James Sweatt		James × Sweatt
	Edward Whittington		Ed × Whittington
	Isom Camble		Isom × Camble
	William Canaday		Wm × Canaday
35	Nathaniel Notts		Nathanel Notts
	Ephram Whittington	44.30	
	Henry Driver		Henry × Driver
	Jacob Summerford		Jacob × Summerford
	James Smith		James × Smith

RECORDS OF THE SOUTH CAROLINA LINE 21

Jarrod Whittington		Jarrod × Whittington
Jihua Rynolds		
Daniel Hill	44.80	Daniel × Hill
Joseph Allison	24.80×	

Pay Roll of Capt. William Caldwell's Company for August, September & October 1779

Rank		Names	Pay & subsistence in Dollars. 90th	Receipts
Captain		William Caldwell	626-	Wm Caldwell
Lieut.		John Jones	333.20	John Jones
Serj^{ts}.	{	Robert Hood	55-	Robert Hood
		Benj^a. Fatherree	55-	Benjamin Fatherree
Corps	{	William Slater	46.82	
		Thomas Clements	46.82	Thomas Clements
Private	1.	John Steward	44.80	John × Steward
	2	Jacob Weaver	44.80	Jacob × Weaver
	3	William Slicker	44.80	
	4	Morris Moore		Morris × Moore
	5	John Main		John × Main
	6	James Smith		
		Aaron Taylor		
		John Tucker		John tucker
		Morris Florida		
		James Killgore		James × Killgore
		William Scott		Wm × Scott
		Owen Richardson		
		Francis Howell		Francis Howell
		William Morris		Wm × Morris
		John Hayes		John × Hayes
		Henry Covington		Henry × Covington
		William Johnson		Wm Johnson
		Benjamin Johnson		Benjn × Johnston
		Roger McKinney		
	20	George Gosling		G. Gossling
	21	Cotleip Stinevender		Cotleip Stinvinder

Capt: William Caldwells Company Cont^d..

Rank		Names	Pay &c	Receipts
Privates		Amt brt forw^d=		
	22	Samuel Bill	44.80	
		Mathew Paul		Mathew × Paul
		Henry Killgore		Henry × Killgore
		John Lefever		John Lefever
		William Edwards		

	Moses Disto		
	Adam Smith		Adam × Smith
	Solomon McGraws		
	John Atkinson		
	Nathaniel Hood		
	Nicholas Rodemeyer		Nicholas × Rodemyer
	John O'Neal	46.20	
	Reuben Copeland	51.50	Reuben Copeland
	John Hunt	48.30	John Hunt
	Randolph Bowers	33.90	
37	Bakie Harvey	33.20	
38	James Whedon	33.20	
		2845.74	

Pay Roll of Capt. Oliver Towles's Company, for August, September & October 1779.

Rank	Names	Pay & Subsistence in Dollars. 90th..	Receipts
Captain	Oliver Towles	626	
Lieut:	John Knapp	333.20	John Knap
Lieut	Merry McGuire	252.30	Merry MGuire
Serjeants	Elias Bridgewater	55.	Elias Bridgewater
	Henry Crum	55.	Henry Crum
	Edmund Chancey	55.	Edmund Chancey
Corporals	Thomas Gill	46.82	thos Gill
	James Bowland	46.82	
	Henry Hutto	46.82	Henry Hutto
Privates 1.	Isaac Bridgewater	44.80	Isaac Bridgewater
2	Michael Cain	44.80	Michl= Cain
3	William Godfrey	44.80	Wm × Godfrey
	John Morning	44.80	John × Morning
	Thomas McDowall	44.80	Thos × McDowall
	Caleb Owens	44.80	Caleb × Owens
	John Fulker		John × Fulker
	Richard Brett		Richard × Brett
	Patrick McCabe		
	William Hanson		William Hinson
	Benjamin Evans		
	Henry Kembler		Henry × Kembler
	John Caldwell		John Caldwell
14	Charles Anthony		

RECORDS OF THE SOUTH CAROLINA LINE 23

Capt. Oliver Towles's Company Cont^d..

Rank Privates	Names Amo^t.. bro^t. forw^d.	Pay &c	Receipts
15	John Looft	44.80	
	Peter Harris	44.80	
	Martin Martin		Martin Martin
	Miles Goodwyn		Miles Gooden
	Jesse Bussby		Jesse Brozbe
	Britton Johnston		Britton X Johnston
	Edward Hughes		Edward X Hughes
	John Cowden		John Coudene
	Bozwell Brown		Bozwell Brown
	James Douglass		James Dougles
	Raymond Jones		Raymond X Jones
	William Davis		William X Davis
	James Jones		James X Jones
	Icabod Balium		
	Moses Livingston		Moses Leviston
	Bartley Adkins		Bart.. X Adkins
	William Ellidge		
	Jonathan Parker		Jon^n.. X Parker
	James Hogg		
	Samuel Cross		Samuel X Cross
	Robert Dunlap		Robert X Dunlap
36	Peter Beaseley		Peter X Beasley
37	Miles Jackson	44.80	

Capt. Oliver Towles's Company Cont^d..

Rank Privates	Names Amo^t.. bro^t. forw^d..	Pay &c	Receipts
38	Andrew Julian	44.80	
39	Thomas Niaurd	44.80	
40	Joseph Yancy	33.20	
41	James Burges	33.20	
		3415.26	

Pay Roll of Capt. Field Farrar's Company for August, September & October 1779.

Rank	Names	Pay & Subsist. in Dollars 90th.	Receipts
Captain	Field Farrar	626	Field Farrar
Serjeants	{ John McMahen	55	John McMehen
	Samuel Ratliffe	55	Samuel Ratliff
	John Scott	55	John Scott

Corporals	Willis Perkins	46.82	Willis × Perkins
	William Paul	46.82	
	Samuel Croft	46.82	
Drum	Wade Blair	46.82	Wade × Blare
Fife	John Mulcaster	46.82	John Mulcaster
Privates 1.	James Dogherty	44.80	James × Dogharty
2	Edward Ellis	44.80	Edward × Ellis
3	Jesse Perkins		Jesse × Perkins
4	Richard Carmichael		Richard × Carmichael
5	Isaac Collier		Isaac Collier
6	Francis Frankum		Francis × Frankum
7	Frederick Heron		Fred^k.. × Heron
8	James Singleton		James × Singleton
9	Ambrose Singleton	44.80	Ambrous Singleton

Capt. Field Farrar's Company Cont^d..

Rank	Names	Pay &c	Receipts
	Amt bro^t. forw^d.		
Privates 10	John Prescott	44.80	John × Prescot
11	John Flick		John Flick
12	Benjamin Prescot		Benj × Prescot
13	Robert Read		Robert × Read
14	Moses Wilson		Moses Wilson
15	Jesse Crowther		Jesse × Crowther
	Malachi McKoy		Malachi × McKoy
	Henry Wilson		Henry Wilson
	Gilbert Groomes		Gilbert × Groomes
	William Chavis		William × Chavis
	John Read		John × Read
	Jacob Brunson		Jacob × Brunston
	John Edens		John × Edens
	James Moates		James × Motes
	John Smith		John × Smith
	James Carter		James × Carter
	Dempsey Perkins		
	James Eggerton		James Eggerton
	Daniel Gibson		Daniel Gibson
	Peter Rasher		Peter × Rasher
	Philip Kearsey		Philip × Kersey
	James Seward		James seward
	Stephen Brown		
	Conrod Rife	44.80	Conrod × Rife
35	George Hart	44.80	
36	John Chavis	33.20	

Capt: Field Farrar's Company Cont^d=

Rank	Names Amo^t: bro^t. fow^d=	Pay &c	Receipts
Privates 37	William James	33.20	
38	Owen Whittenton	33.20	
		2696.30	

Pay Roll of Capt. George Liddell's Company for August, September & October 1779

Rank	Names	Pay & Subsistence in Dollars 90th.	Receipts
Captain	George Liddell	626	Geo. Liddell
Lieut.	James Robison	286.70	Ja^s. Robison
Serj^{ts}..	James McDaniell	55	James M^{c}denniel
	William Woodford	55	William Wodford
	Bartley Wharton	55	
Corp^s.	Daniel Shanon	46.82	Daniel Shannon
	Samuel Foxworth	46.82	Samuel Foxworth
Fife	Samuel Brushears	46.82	Saml. X Brushears
Privates 1	Matthew Johnson	44.80	Mathew X Johnston
	Ambrose Jackson		Ambros X Jackson
	John Price		John Price
	Theophilus Norwood		
	Thomas Price		Thomas Price
	Benjamin Holley		Benj: X Holley
	Morgan Griffin		Morgan X Griffin
	Berry Jeffers		Berry X Jeffers
	Gideon Griffin		Gideon X Griffen
10	Osborn Jeffers	44.80	Osborn X Jeffers.

Capt: George Liddell's Company Cont^d=

Rank	Names Amo^t.. bro^t. fow^d..	Pay &c	Receipts
Privates 11.	Allen Jeffers	44.80	Allan Jeffers
	Benjamin Culpepper		Benjn. X Culpepper
	George Harrison	33.20 X	
	Jacob Miller	44.80	Jacob Miller
	Michael Powell		Michael X Powell
	Isaac Carey		
	Dreury Harris		Dreury X Harris
	James Keenan		James Keenenen
	Peter McGrew		Peter X McGrew
	John Winn		John Wynn

	Names	Pay &c	Receipts
	John Dyer		J D°yer
	Samuel Russ		
	Samuel Shaw		Samuel Shaw
	Thomas Wood		Michael Morgan
	Michael Morgan		Thomas Woods
	Reuben Powell		
	Henry Foster		
	James Carter		James × Carter
	Abraham Miller		Abrah^m.. × Miller
	William Thomson		
31	John Bussby		John × Busby
32	Thomas Smith		Thomas × Smith
33	Samuel Anderson		Samuel × Anderson
34	Edward Williamson	44.80	Edward × Williamson

Capt: George Liddells Company Cont^d..

Rank	Names	Pay &c	Receipts
	Amo^t.. bro^t.. fow^d=		
Privates 35	Samuel Windsor	44.80	Saml × Windsor
36	Britton Goodwyn	44.80	Britton × Goodwyn
37	William Bryan		
38	Thomas Sutherland		Thomas × Sotherland
39	Paul Green		Paul × Green

Pay Roll of Capt. John Henington's Company for August, September & October 1779.

Rank	Names	Pay &c	Receipts
Captain	John Heninton	626	John Heninton
Lieut.	Robert Gaston	333.20	
Serjeants {	David O'Harra	55	David Ohara
	Robert Ritchie	55	
Corporals {	Edward Lane	46.82	
	Solomon Peters	"	
	John Cook	"	John Cook
Drum^r:	Elijah Johnson	"	Elijah × Johnston
Fife	Jeremiah Davis	46.82	Jerem^h.. × Davis
Privates 1.	Lewis Neal		Lewis × Neal
2	Richard Ward		Richard × Ward
	Thomas Douglass		Thomas × Douglas
	James Draper		James × Draper
	Joseph Freeman		Joseph × Freeman
6	Taylor Holloway	44.80	Taylor Holloway

RECORDS OF THE SOUTH CAROLINA LINE

Capt: John Henintons Company cont[d]..

Rank		Names	Pay &c	Receipts
		Amot.. brot.. fow[d]..		
Privates	7.	Josiah Harper	44.80	Josiah Harper
		Samuel Hutson		Saml Hutson
		Jesse Hinson		Jesse X Henson
		Joseph James	33.20	
		John Jones	44.80	John Jones
		Abraham Johnson	44.80	
		William Knighton		Wm X Knighton
		Anthony Lauson		Anthony Lauson
		Benjamin Lane		Benj X Lane
		William Myrick		Wm X Myrick
		Jacob Myers		
		William Partridge		Wm X Partridge
		John Parish		
	21	Anthony Pool		Anthony Pooll
	22	Uriah Porter		
	23	James Quarles		
		Samuel Quarles		Samuel Quarels
	24	Gilbert Rollison		Ja[s].. Quarles
		Henry Grigory		Henry X Griggoray
		William Sanders		
		George Shepherd		George X Shepherd
		John Smith		John X Smith
		William Young		
		Henry Fulk		
		John Isaacs		
	32	Isiah Moore		
	33	Nicholas Meigler		

Capt: John Heninton's Company cont[d].

Rank		Names	Pay &c	Receipts
		Amot.. Brot.. Forw[d]=		
Privates	34	Robert Rotten	44.80	Robert X Routten
		Lamuel Robertson	44.80	Lamuel X Robinson
		Henry Smith	44.80	
		Benjamin Thomson	33.20	
	38	Nicholas Powers	44.80	

2965.10

Pay Roll of Field & Staff Officers for August, September & October 1779.

Rank	Names	Pay & Subsistence in Dollars 90th..	Receipts
Colonel	William Thomson	1489.15	W^m.. Thomson
Lt Colonel	James Mayson	1191.30	
Major	Samuel Wise	652.	
Surgeon	James Martin	939.	John James Haig Exor[7] Jam. Martin
Pay Master	John James Haig	180.	John James Haig
Adjutant	Merry McGuire	99.	Merry Mguire
		4550.45	

Account of Cash Received of Joseph Clay Esqr. Dep. Pay Mast. Genl.. for Augt. Sept & Octob. 1779.

	Field & Staff Officer's Roll			4550.45
	1.	Felix Warley's	Do	3628.10
	2	David Hopkins's	Do	2634.66
	3	John C. Smiths	Do	2825.56
Captains	4	Joseph Warley's	Do	2901.....
	5	Uriah Goodwyn's	Do	3561.22
	6	William Caldwells	Do	2845.74
	7	Oliver Towles	Do	3415.26
	8	Field Farrar's	Do	2696.30
	9	George Liddell's	Do	2929.66
	10	John Henington's	Do	2965.10
				34953.45

---

[7] Executor must have been used here in the sense of agent or attorney, as Dr. Martin did not die until 1797.

RECORDS OF THE SOUTH CAROLINA LINE

Pay Roll of Capt: Felix Warley's Company for Continental & State Pay, vizt

Rank	Names	Continental Pay & Subsistence for Nov: 1779	Additional pay of the State for Sept. Octo^r & Nov: 1779	Receipts
		Dollars		
Captain	Felix Warley	240	78	Felix Warley
Lieut:	Lewis DeSaussure		50	D DeSaussure admr^a
Serg Maj.	Isaac Vaughan		20 39	Isaac Vaughan
Q M. Serj.	Robert Johnston		20.33	Robt. Johnston

[Here follow the names of the men of F. Warley's company, as already given, and next, in order, similar pay-rolls of the companies of Hopkins, Smith and Joseph Warley, on the latter of which the name of John Goodwyn appears as second lieutenant.]

Pay Roll of Field & Staff Officers of the 3^d.. Reg^t.. for Continental & State Pay vizt..

Rank	Names	Continental Pay & Subsist for Novr. 1779	Additional Pay of the State for Septr. Oct^r.. & Nov 1779.	Receipts
Colonel	William Thomson	575	168	
Lt Colonel	James Mayson	460	156	
Major	Samuel Wise		44.18^b	
Surgeon	James Martin	360	30.	John James Haig Exr Jam Martin
Lt & Adjt..	Merry McGuire	33	153.	Merry Mguire
Pay Master	John James Haig	60	60.	John James Haig
		1488.	611.18	

^{a}Louis de Saussure was mortally wounded at Savannah, October 9, 1779.
^{b}Wise was killed at Savannah, October 9, 1779, and his estate doubtless got no Continental pay for November.

Account of Cash received of Joseph Clay Esquire Dep: Pay Mast^r: Genl. . for Novem. 1779 being for the Contien Pay & Subsistance; And also for cash received of the Treasurers for Septem^r. October & Nov: 1779 being the State Pay allowed the 3^d.. Regt

	Field & Staff Officers'	Roll	1488	. . .	611.18
	1 Felix Warley's	Do	1061		1128.72
	2 David Hopkins'.	Do	974.60		831.
	3 John C. Smith's	Do	1030.40		909.72
	4 Joseph Warleys	Do	1059.30		1020.36
Captains	5 Uriah Goodwyn's	Do	1145.30		1042.
	6 William Caldwell's	Do	1233.40		898.
	7 Oliver Towles's	Do	1053.80		899.
	8 Field Farrar's	Do	997.		882.
	9 George Liddell's	Do	1186.30		968.72
	10 John Henington's	Do	1043.30		974.
			12272.7		10162. 6

[14]

[COL. C. C. PINCKNEY TO MAJOR ISAAC HARLESTON.]

Addressed: Major Harleston—

Dear Major,
    I had yesterday a severe fit of the fever, but am better this afternoon. I enclose you a Letter from Mathews to me which came by the Flag, after having perused it, pray return it. Do acquaint us if the fleet has made any movements and if it is known who they are; don't fail to acquaint us by the return of the Boy for we acknowledge we are anxious.

                Yrs sincerely
           Charles Cotesworth Pinckney
                         Oct 29

RECORDS OF THE REGIMENTS OF THE SOUTH CAROLINA LINE, CONTINENTAL ESTABLISHMENT.

[15.]

[A ROSTER OF OFFICERS OF THE 6th REG^{t}.[10]]

---

[10]This roster and the two following appear on three pages of a folio sheet from a book. It was evidently a brigade roster or order book and this fragment is all that has been preserved of it.

Roster of the Officers of the 6th—Regiment Apl. 15, 1779

Captains	Guard	Camp Piquet	Command	G=C=Martial	B—C—Martial	R. C=Martial	Fatigue
Taylor	Command		Apl 13			June 5th 1779	
Doggett	G C: Ml:			April 15th. 79		June 5th 1779[11]	
Warley	Apl: 14 do= 19th=	Apl 21					
Boyes	Absent with leave						
Hampton	April 15. 1779 do. 22d	Apl 30					
Buchanan		Apl. 18		Apl. 13		Apl. 21	
Baker	Absent with Leave						
Lieutenants							
Pollard						June 5th 1779[11]	
Brown	Apl: 13 May 2d do= 19th=					Apl 21	
Adair	Apl 22d	Apl: 16 May 1st	Apl: 6				
Doggett	Apl. 16 Apl 23	Apl. 20				Apl. 21	
Langford	On Command Apl 25	Apl. 23d	Apl.. 13				

[11] See page 87 of the April issue of this magazine.

RECORDS OF THE SOUTH CAROLINA LINE   33

[16.]

[A GUARD ROSTER OF THE 1ST. AND 6TH. REGTS.]

Roster of 1st: & 6th: Reg=for Guard December. 1779.

Capts..Theus		G. Ct. Martial	Garison Cts. Mart
Warley		I	I
Elliott	decemr Jany 17 31st— 24	I	IIII
Hext		I	II
Lining	Jany Jany 8 do 18 1—1780 13th= 25	II	IIII
Hampton		I	IIII
Buchanan	26 Decr Jany 7 23 Jany 2d— 19 1780	I	IIII
Baker	Decemr Jany 9 20 27th 14 28	I	IIII
Gadsden	Jany 4 29	0	I
Williamson	Decr 28 Jany 10 30 3d Jany 21	I	III
Pollard	decr 29 Jany 5 Jany 15 11th 22d	I	II
Levacher—	Decr Jany 6 Jany 12 23d 30 16th	I	II
Brown			II
Fishburn			
Skirving			
Lts Langford	Decr. Decemr Jany 7 Jany 22d 26th 31st II 17th 26	I	IIII
Bradwell	27 Jany 28th 1st 1780 Jany 7 Jany 22d 3d Jany 11th 27	I	III
Parham			II
Buchanan	Qur.. Mastr.		
Ward	Decr 28 Jany 1st Jany 8 Jany 15 23d. 3d Jany 12th Sick 27		II
Hazard	Decr. Jany 5 Jany 12 Jany 19 28 29 ditto 8 15th 23d:		I
Brown	Decr Decem Jany 5 Jany 9 Jany 15 24 26th 29 13th 19 28 29		II
Doyley	Decem ditto Jany 6 Jany 9 Jany 16 24 4 26th.. 30— 13th— 20 29		II
Wm: Ward	Decr. 27. do 29 Jany 6 Jany 10 Jany 16 25 4 14th 20 29		
Petrie	31st. decr. Jany Jany 10 Jany 17 25 30 14th 21		
Kennedy	Jany 21 30 26		

[17.]

[A PARTIALLY DESTROYED ROSTER.]

A Roster of [obliterated] Regiments [obliterated] Feby 28. 1780.

Captains
Mazyck
Jo Warley
Goodwyn
G Warley
Baker[12]
Buchanan
Baker 3d[13]
Mason
Turner
Gray
Pollard

Lieutenants
Langford
Smith
Evans
Buchanan
Mazyck[14]

[18.]

[REPORT OF COURT OF INQUIRY ON LIEUT. FRASER.]

(Here Insert the Genl. Order for the Court's Sitting.)

January 12th 1780

Pursuant to the above Order the Court met this Day
Presid^t. Major Harleston
Members Captains Elliott & Buchanan
Lieutenants Langford & Bradwell
The Court for want of Evidence Adjourned 'till Tomorrow 10. oClock The Court met Accord^g to Adjournm^t. no Evi-

---

[12]Richard Bohun Baker. [13]Jesse Baker, of the 3d. Regiment.
[14]The records accompanying these names are all obliterated.

dence appearing adjourned 'till Tomorrow & from Day to Day afterwards to
January 16. 1780
The Evidences attending The Court [word or two obliterated] proceeded to the Examination of Captain Jacob Milligan [several words obliterated] about to quit the Vessel he looked to see [word or two obliterated] could bring [two or three words obliterated] the wounded when he discovered Lieut. Fraser below, without the Crescent on his Cap but that he did not see him in the Action on [undecipherable word] as he recollects
Jn°. Milligan says that in the heat of the Action he saw L^t. Fraser below, with the Crescent out of his Cap
W^m- Bishop says that Capt Milligan at the Commencem^t. of the Action had Ordered the Hold to be open for the reception of the wounded when he observed M^r. Fraser go down—& that he never saw him again on Deck—
Qu When you saw him on Deck did he appear possest of himself—
An—He did not appear disconcerted & went leisurely down the Hold—but never returned again on Deck while he was on board
Capt M. again called—Qu—Did you not say that L^t. Fraser desired to know when on board if you intended to fight in y^r. uniform
An—Yes. He did ask me & my answer was I would & if killed should be in them—Capt M. being asked if M^r. Fraser appeared Calm th° Confused—He Answered he thought he did
L^t. Fraser produced on his defence The Depositions of Jn° Davis— Th°. Jones Richard Martin Mariners—see the Depositions—adding that he did not at any time go down into the Hold but remained on Deck & that he assisted one of the wounded near his Station
The Court after full Consideration of the Evidence pro-

duced is of opinion that Lieutenant Fraser is a subject for a General Court Martial

[19.]

[COL. C. C. PINCKNEY TO MAJ. ISAAC HARLESTON.]

Addressed: Major Harleston
Fort Moultrie/

Charlestown Jan: 20: 1780
Dear Major,
The Governor will send twenty Militia to augment the Garrison, you will be so good as to accommodate them in the best manner, and as soon as they arrive send a party of a serjeant & Nine regulars to Dewees's Island to serve as a covering party there to the Negroes who are to cut wood for the Garrison. I hope you received twelve Cords of wood the day before yesterday I was surprised to find from a Letter of Major De Brahm to Col[1]: Laumoy that some of the soldiers have died for the want of Medicines & Necessaries in the Hospital, as D[r]: Orr may have whatever supplies He thinks requisite on only taking the trouble to apply to the General Hospital. I have not received a Letter from my Brother[15] since I saw you, but Phil Neyle tells me that he is exceedingly reduced by the flux & is now giving the Beaume de Vie a fair tryal. My Mother[16] writes me he is very poorly. I mentioned to you I believe that I had neither seen nor heard from Col[1]: Scott, but am informed that he will be at the Fort tomorrow. Marion, Henderson & Scott are our Lieutenant Colonels;

---

[15]Major Thomas Pinckney.
[16]Mrs. Eliza (Lucas) Pinckney, widow of Hon. Charles Pinckney, sometime chief-justice of South Carolina.

Pinckney, Harleston & Hyrne our Majors.[17] I do not congratulate you on your appointment because I know you wished for an Honorable opportunity of retiring to the Class of a private Citizen, but I congratulate my Country on the assurance we now have of not losing your abilities in the Field during the Continuance of the present war. I shall write you more fully tomorrow at present Davis waits for my Letter. I beg my love to the officers & remain
      Yrs sincerely
      Charles Cotesworth Pinckney—
I am obliged to you for your favor of yesterday.

[20.]

[GEORGE ABBOTT HALL TO MAJOR ISAAC HARLESTON.]

Addressed: [Torn off] aac Harleston
      at
      Fort Moultrie

Dear Sir
  I have occasions for 5 m feet 2 Inch 5 m feet Inch & half & 5 m feet Inch & quarter pine plank, for a Vessel to load, can You supply me with that Quantity, & when, for which the *Cash* shall be immediately paid on delivery. I should be glad of your answer as soon as possible, either to M^r. Corbetts (where I write this with a bad pen as you may see) or if the Coxswain knows my House to be sent there —I am with regard
      Dr Sir

Can you let me have also	Y^r Very hble Servt.
20 to 25 bbls Tarr &	Geo. Abbott Hall
100 bls Turpentine	24th. January 1780—

---

[17]He evidently knew before the publication by Gen. Lincoln of his order of February 11, 1780, consolidating the five infantry regiments of South Carolina into three, what officers were to be retained in active service. (See the order in Vol. III. of this magazine, pp. 177-179.)

[21.]

[COL. C. C. PINCKNEY TO MAJ. ISAAC HARLESTON.]

Addressed: Major Harleston
or the Commanding officer
at
Fort Moultrie/

Charlestown. Jan 27: 1780=
Dear Major,
The signals of the French Frigates are a Dutch Flag at the Main mast—
If the Enemy are upon the Coast a Blue Flag at the Main Mast.
Please to add to your Estimate of Plank the Quantity which will be necessary the repair the Planks in the Fort immediately h'ow the guns are, and [undecipherable word] place the Plank at [undecipherable word] Guard, and make each note separate.
The General has informed me that the voice of the majority of the Regiments were that the Captains to fill up the three retained regiments should be appointed by the Field Officers after the Field officers had been elected by the Governor and himself and that they had accordingly agreed that the three regiments should be commissioned by the following Field Officers, viz.

1st Reg { Col^l: Pinckney
L^t: Col^l: Scott
Major Pinckney—

2^d: Reg^t: { L^t: Col^l: Marion
Major Harleston

3^d: Reg^t: { Col^l: Thompson
L^t: Col^l: Henderson (if he will accept, if not,
L^t: Col^l: Horry)
Major Hyrne

The General has ordered me to collect the sentiments of the said F: officers with respect to the Captains for filling up the line as soon as possible. To each regiment there are to be Nine Captains now appointed. I shall be therefore glad to receive your sentiments on the above subject by the very first opportunity. For my own part, I think the mode least liable to exception, will be to appoint the 27 Captains who have been longest in Service. I don't mean the 27 Eldest Captains, but the 27 oldest officers who have now the rank of Captain, as I think those officers who have been perhaps three years in the service or more, and who have but lately obtained the rank of Captain are entitled to be preferred on account of their long service to those who tho' Senior Captains have not been in the Service altogether above a year or two. But these are only my private sentiments on this Matter, and I shall be happy to receive yours without delay. When Col[1]: Scott arrives, be so good as to shew him this Letter and tell him, I shall be glad to receive his sentiments on the same subject.

    Yrs sincerely
      Charles Cotesworth Pinckney—

RECORDS OF THE REGIMENTS OF THE SOUTH CAROLINA LINE, CONTINENTAL ESTABLISHMENT.

[22.]

[MAJOR DE BRAHM TO MAJOR HARLESTON.]

Addressed: To
Major Harleston
of the 6th- S. C. Regm^t.
Commanding at
Fort Moultrie

DIMENSIONS FOR A PLATFORM.

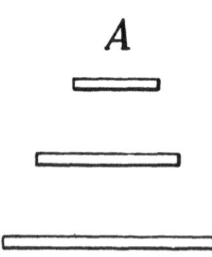 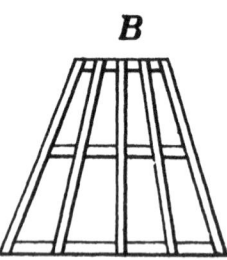 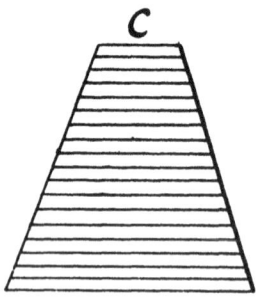

A. Is the first Foundation of a Platform, for which are required three Joists, the first 8 Feet long, the 2^d. 12¼. & the last 16½ each by 10 Inches thick—

B. for the second Course, for which are required 5. Joists more all 18 Feit long and 6 by 4, or thereabouts thik. further

C. if the Plancks are a Foot broad, 18 of them, of which the first must be 9 Feet long, the next 9½ the next 10, the next 10½ the next 11 & so on.

they must be upwards of two Inches thik

M^r. de Brahm presents his Comp^s. to Maj. Harleston, & sends him this short Information ab^t. Platforms for want of Time to be more explicit ab^t. it, but hopes it will be sufficient—Sapienti pauca—

Maj. Harleston will be so good, as to employ the few Negroes left at the Island for his & the garrisons benefit, as he pleases—

Jan. 30, 1780—

[23.]

[A RETURN OF THE 2D. REGIMENT.]

Monthly Return of the Second Regiment of South Carolina Infantry Commanded by Lieutenant Colonel Francis Marion Comm^t. January 31st—1780

	Officers fit for duty									Non Commissioned								Rank & file						Wants to Comp^t		Alterations Since Last Return						Joined
	Lieut Colonel	Major	Captains	Subalterns	Adjutant	Qr. Master	Pay Master	Surgeon	Mates	Serjt. Major	Qr. M. Serjeant	Fife Major	Drum Major	Serjt. fit for Duty	Serjt. on furlough	Serjt. Sick Absent	Drums & fifes	Fit for Duty	Sick Present	Sick Absent	on Command	on furlough	Total	Serjeants	Drums & fifes	Dead	Deserted	Discharged	Serjts.	Dr & fifes	R & file	
Field & Staff	1	„	„	„	1	1	1	1	1	1	1	1	1	„	„	„	„	„	„	„	„	„	„	„	„	„	„	„	„	„	„	
Light Infantry	„	„	1	1	„	„	„	„	„	„	„	„	„	2	1	„	2	26	3	5	4	5	43	„	32	„	„	„	„	„	1	
Capt Moultry	„	„	1	„	„	„	„	„	„	„	„	„	„	2	1	„	2	6	„	7	8	1	22	„	53	„	„	„	„	„	„	
„ Mazyck	„	„	1	1	„	„	„	„	„	„	„	„	„	2	1	„	2	17	3	4	2	„	26	„	49	„	2	„	„	„	„	
„ Proveaux	„	„	1	„	„	„	„	„	„	„	„	„	„	2	„	„	2	9	3	3	3	3	20	1	55	„	1	„	„	„	1	
„ Mason	„	„	1	1	„	„	„	„	„	„	„	„	„	2	„	„	2	8	5	2	7	1	23	1	52	„	„	„	„	„	1	
„ Gray	„	„	1	„	„	„	„	„	„	„	„	„	„	2	„	„	2	7	7	5	3	„	22	1	53	„	2	„	„	„	„	
„ Roux	„	„	1	„	„	„	„	„	„	„	„	„	„	2	„	„	2	11	3	3	4	„	26	1	53	„	„	„	„	„	„	
1st Vacant	„	„	„	1	„	„	„	„	„	„	„	„	„	1	„	„	2	15	4	4	4	„	26	2	49	„	1	„	„	„	„	
2d Vacant	„	„	„	„	„	„	„	„	„	„	„	„	„	1	„	„	2	11	3	5	2	„	21	2	54	„	2	„	„	„	„	
	1	„	6	4	„	„	„	1	1	1	1	1	1	16	3	„	18	110	32	35	37	11	225	8	450	„	8	„	„	„	„	

Vacant
Sick Present

RECORDS OF THE SOUTH CAROLINA LINE

Absent Officers

Names	from When	By whose Leave	Place whare	Time of Absence	Reasons
Capt Moultrie	7th Decr.	Lt. Colo Marion	Chas. Town	20 Days	on Duty
" Mazyck	8th do.	do	do		
" Mason	7th do	do	do	15	Sick
" Gray	15 Octr	do	do		Wounded
" Roux	9th do	do	do		P: W: on Parole
Lieut. Martin	4th Novr	Colo Marion	Country		
" Kolb	8th Decr.	do	Chas. Town	15 Days	
" Legire	12th Decmr	do	Country		Sick

From the 5th & 6th Regt. added to the 2d. { Captains Geo Warley Decr 26. 1777
Thomas Shubrick
Lieuts—Danl Langford
John Frierson
Geo. Evans

Resigned
Capt. Rich'd Baker..............Capt Thos. Hall
Lt. William Capers..............Lt Alexr. Petrie

Dates of Commissions

Lieut. Colo. Francis Marion Sept. 16......1776
Major John Vanderhorst Oct. 9 1779
Capt. Thomas Moultrie October 2d. 1776
Daniel Mazyck May 6th. 1777
Adrien Proveaux April 27th. 1778
Richard Mason Novr- 25th. 1778
Peter Gray Decemr- 29. 1778
Albert Roux August 4th 1779
Lieut. John Martin
" Peter Fossine July 18th- 1778
" Josiah Kolb July 15th- 1778
" George Ogier August 4th. 1779
" James Legare Oct- 9th. 1779

Pay Master Henry Gray
Surgeon Jeremiah Theus August 2d. 1777
Surgeon Mate Silvester Springer June 27th. 1778

Officers who have joined the Second Regiment under the late Regulation in February 1780—

of the 5th
——————
{ Captain Thomas Shubrick.. Commission bearing Date
Lieutenants George Evans
John Frierson }

6th..
{ Captain George Warley
Lieutenant Dan¹=Langford }

[24.]

[WILLIAM MASSEY TO COMMANDANT AT HADDRELL'S POINT.]

Addressed: To
The Commandant
at
Haddrell's Point

Sir—It is General Lincoln's desire that all the Troops at Haddrell's Point & Fort Moultrie be forthwith muster'd—you will please therefore to give out in Orders that three Muster Rolls of each Company of every Regiment be made out ready by Tuesday the 15th- Febry- next when the Troops will be muster'd, and to the end, that no time may be lost, in making my returns of the said Muster I request to direct that the Rolls be sworn to before the Commandant immediately after the Muster is taken—
Sir,
Your most hble Servt
Wm Massey D. M. G.

Charles Town
1 [break] Feb 1780-

Endorsed: Orders by Major Harleston
That 3 Muster Rolls of each
[Rest undecipherable.]

[25.]

[JOSIAH DUPONT TO LT.-COL. WILLIAM HENDERSON.]

Addressed: Col^l- Henderson

23 Feb^r- 1780-

Sir/
 Mr Davice Calls on me for Beef for the publick wh [break] am Ready to furnish, at Same time Shall be oblige to you to See me Satisfyed for s^d Beef, I laid my Book before Mr Davice that he m [break] asure you of the price which I have obtained for my Beef which are [break] for the fore Qu^{rs}- & 65/ for the Hinds—I am sir Y^r H [break]
Josiah Dupont

[26.]

[FRANCIS COBIA TO MAJOR ISAAC HARLESTON.]

Rec^d March 22 ^{the} 1780 of Mager Isaac Harlston twenty head of oxen & seaven head of steers for the use of the Publick Fran^s Cobia

[27.]

[RUM, SUGAR AND COFFEE REPORT OF THE 2D REGT.]

An Account of Rum Shugar & Coffe Deliverd the Officers of 2^{d}Regt. at Sheldon—

1779			Rum	Shugar	Coffee
17 Nov^r-	Col^o.	Marion	3¼	15	10
	Captn.	Moultrie	3¼	15	10
		Mazyck	1	9	3
		Hall Del^d. Captn Mason	2½		
		Dunbar	4	9	3
		Baker	1		
		Proveaux	13	40	25
		Mason	2½	9	3
	L^t	Capers	14		
		Foissin. Deliv^d- L^t- Kolb	3	24	3
		Kolb	4	9	3
		Ogier	15½	30	6
		Lagare	2	9	3
		Rogers	4	9	3
	D^r	Theus	4	41	11
1780-		Springer S. M	2	41	11
2^d Feby:	Captn.	Moultrie	3½		
	Col	Marion	5		
	Captn.	Proveaux	4		
	L^t.	Foissin	2		
	L^t	Ogier	1		
	L^t	Foissin	1½	5	
		Ogier	1½		
		Silv. Springer	1		
March.	Col^o	Marion	2¾	6	2
	Captn	Moultrie... at Bacon Bridge	2¾	6	2
		Preveaux..	2¾	6	2
	L^t	Lagare......	1		
		Ogier........	1		
	Col^o.	Marion	6½		
21 March	Captn	Proveaux	6½		
			119¾	255	

			Rum	Shugar	Coffee
Rum Shugar & Coffee Del^d the 2^d Regt Brought Over					
	Maj^r.	Vanderhorst	16		
	Captn	Moultrie...	4		
	L^t	Lagare....... in town	5		
	L^t	Foissin......	10	15	5
	Captn.	Baker.......	7	30	
			161¾	45	
		Brought over	*	*	*
		Total	161*	*	*
	Captn.	Mazyck		2	22
31st.	L^t	Evance	4	5	
	Col^o.	Marion	3	5	
	L^t.	Ogier, order on Capt^{ns} Martin & Lagare Delivered him	3		
31st			1	*	16
	Maj^r.	Vanderhorst at Sheldon	*	10	*
			..*	*	*
	Lt	Hart Del^d Newton 1^s p^r. V. ord^r.			
	Col^o.	Marion			

* Figures undecipherable.

RECORDS OF THE REGIMENTS OF THE SOUTH CAROLINA LINE, CONTINENTAL ESTABLISHMENT.

[28.]

[OFFICERS OF THE 2ND. REGIMENT, 1780.]

Major Harleston—Decr. 30th.. 1778—
Capt^s. Mazyck—May 6th.. 1777—
Warley—Decr 26th. 1777—
Shubrick
Baker—April 25th. 1778
Proveau— 27—1778
Mason—Nov^r: 25th.. 1778—
Gray—Decr. 30th.. 1778—

Foissin—July 13th.. 1778
Kolb— 15th.. 1778
Langford—Octr. 3^d. 1778—
Frierson March-9th..1779—
Evanes—Aug: 18th. 1779
Ogier— 4.. 79—
Legare—Oct^r: 9 1779
Dunbar—Feb: 24th.. 1780
Hart— 28- —1780
Mazyck—March —— 1780
Mazyck
Pay Master Gray—
Jer^h: Theus—Aug: 2^d. 1777
Mate Syl: Springer—June 27th-. 1778—

47

[29.]

[RUM AND SUGAR RETURNS OF THE 2ND. REGIMENT.]

A rum return for the Officers of the 2^d. S^o. Carolina Reg^t. from March the $20^{th}=$ to $Ap^l=$ 18 Both Inclusive 1780

1 Colonel
1 Major............................ 30 jells
7 Captains........................210 -d°.
7 Lieutenants............ ....210 -d°.
1 Paymaster..................... 30 -d°.
2 Surgeon & Mate.............. 60 -d°.
  ──────
  540 jells

Captains to Draw Rum & Sugar   Rum due from $20^{th}=$ March & Sugar from Ap^l. 10th

Capt. Moultrie		Subalterns
Mazyck		
Warley		Foissin
Baker		Kolb
Provaux	Gill a day due from 10th & Sugar also—	Langford
Mason		
Gray		Foissin joined Ap^l 12
		Ogier
		Evans
		Legare
		Dunbar
		Hart
		Mazyck
9 Gills Langford		
8 Gills—Frierson		

[30.]

[A RETURN OF THE SICK OF THE 2ND. REGIMENT.]

A Weekly Return of y̆ᵉ. Sick in yᵉ. 2ᵈ. Regᵗ. of South Carolina Infantry Commanded by Col. Frˢ. Marion

Diseases—	Diarrhea	Sore Legs & C—	Intᵍ. Fevers—	Venereal—	Rheumatᶜ. Compˡˢ—	Convalescent	Sent to Gˡ. Hospˡ—	Dischᵈ. fit for Duty	Total—
Total—	2	4	4	1	2	7	3	3	26

April—23ᵈ. 1780— Jh: Theus—Surgⁿ. 2ᵈ Regᵗ-

[31.]

[CHARGE AT A COURT MARTIAL.]

At a Regᵗ. Court Martial held 23ᵈ. April 1780 by order Maj Harleston

Capᵗ. Moultrie, President
Lieuᵗˢ. Ogier & Legaré, Members.

Prisoner, Abraham Anderson confined by Majʳ. Harleston on suspicion of Theft from Peter Lappin

[32.]

[ROSTER OF THE OFFICERS OF THE 2ND. REGIMENT.]

Captains	Guard	Command	General C. Martial	Brigade Ct^s=Martial	Regimental Courts Martial	Fatigue	Piquet
Moultrie	sick Apl 15	Killed	the 24th.	April 1780	Apl 15	Apl 6	
Mazyck	25th Apl 16					19	23
Warley						20	18
Shubrick			Mar 29				
Baker							19
Provaux	Apl 7					22	20
Mason							21
Gray							22
Roux							
Subalterns.							
Martin	Prisnr			Apl 15			
Foissin	20th Abst. Apl. 13=		Mar 29	Apl 15		19	22
Kolb							18
*						20	23
Ogier	22	24	Apl 5				
Frierson	23						19
Evans						22	20
Legare							
Dunbar						sick	
Hart	Adjutant						
Mazyck							21st=
*Langford	Apl 12						

[33.]

[BRIGADE ORDERS, MAY 1, 1780.]

B. O.

The Commanding Officers of the Several Batteries on the Lines are requested to send the returns for the Supply of Ammunition every Morning by Nine OClock as mentioned in the Orders of 25th. Ap^l.—those who are regardless of Orders and this particular point of duty, on wch. not only their own post; but also the Safety of the whole Garrison depends, must expect to be reported to the General
Lieutenant Coll°. Grimke's Corps will furnish constantly an Orderly Serjeant to attend at the Horn Work & be relieved Every Morning at Guard Mounting   May 1st. 1780

[34.]

[ALEXANDER M^{c}QUEEN TO MAJOR HARLESTON.]

Gen: Moultrie will be obliged to Maj: Harleston to order a Serj^t: & twelve Privates to take in charge [break] from Captain [break] battery to [break of several words] Captain [break] battery

A: M^c: Queen
A: de Camp

May 6th, 80,

[35.]

[A RECEIPT FOR ARTILLERY STORES.]

Received May 1st. 1780. from Lieut. Coll^o. Grimke the following Artillery Stores at Battery N° 4—
1—18 pounder on field Carriage
1— 4 pounder–a field piece
30 Cartridges ready filled, including one in the Gun—
57 round Ball & Rammer 1 Apron 1 saddle
4 Grape Shott includ^g one charged
2½ bbs Cannon powder of ' each
¼th Keg priming powder
2 powder Horns & prickers
  Wadding for 18^t=
    18 round Shott
3 Cases fixed Ammunition for brass top d° above
  3 Cases ditto d°. Canister 63 Rounds
  Tubes & portfires—2 Linstocks
  1 Spunge Staff for 4^t= pounder

[36.]

[LT.-COL. HENDERSON TO MAJOR HARLESTON.]

Addressed: Maj Harleston
2 Regim^t–

D Maj.

Capt Coronat is not in Camp, I Coseave you at full Liberty To send the Spades as it was a Genl order.

from D Maj your Hum
Sert
W^m. Henderson

2 May 1780

[37.]

[SUGAR AND COFFEE ISSUED TO 2D. REGIMENT.]

		Sugar. lb.	Coffee lb.
Delivered Capt.	Mazyck	34	25
D°.	Dunbar	9.	25
D°.	Baker	30.	25.
D°.	Provaux	46.	25
D°.—	Mason	9.—	3
D°.—	Gray	50.	25
D°.	Roux	50.	25
D°.	Martin	—	25
D°—	Capers	50.	25
D°—	Petrie	50.	25
D°-	Warley	50.	25
D°-	Kolb	9.	3
D°.	Foissin	44.	11
D°.	Ogier	30.	6
D°.	Legare	9.	18
D°.	Evans	15-	—
D°.	Hart	8.	4
D°.	Theus	41.	11
D°.	Springer	41.	11.

rec^d. from Coll. Marion's house May 3^d. 1780—[18] about 35^{lb} Sugar & 12^{lb} Coffee——

[38.]

[GEN. LINCOLN TO MAJOR HARLESTON.]

Chas-Town May 11. 1780

Sir

You will please to give to Col°. Grimkee Such number of men from the battery you have in charge as he shall call for

I am D Sir your Obdt Servt

B Lincoln

Maj Harleston

---

[18] May 3rd. could not have been the date of the preparing of the above report, for there are names thereon of officers who had resigned before that date.

[39.]

[A RETURN OF THE OFFICERS OF THE 3D. REGT.]

Return of the officers in 3ᵈ. Sᵒ. C. regᵗ

Capᵗˢ— F. Warley...............Servants...............0
       J. C. Smith...............John Peterkin
       J. Warley ....Joˢ. Haynes
       U. Goodwyn............Wᵐ. Chapman
       J. Buchanan............Jnᵒ. Campbell
       J Baker..................Jaˢ. White
       F Farrer.................Jacᵇ.. Brunsin
       G. Liddell................................
       Rᵈ. Pollard...............Wm. Myrack
Lieuts. J. Goodwyn.............Samˡ. Kelley—
       A. Smith...............Peter M Grew
       M. MGuire...............Elijh. MGuire
       Wᵐ. Love .... Thoˢ- Douglas
  Dʳ. Jaˢ. Martin...............Jnᵒ- Cauldwell

    Officers—14   Servants—12
                            Taylor—— 1

                            Tctal 13

2ᵈ June 1780
Felix Warley Capt. Com.
   3 Regᵗ

[40.]

[CAPT. GEORGE TURNER TO MAJOR HARLESTON.]

Addressed: Major Harleston
of the 2ᵈ. Rᵗ· So. Caro=
Haddrell's Point

Dear Sir,
I have laid your Request before Genˡ. Paterson, the Commandant, who tells me he cannot *yet* grant the Indulgence you wish for—but will consider of it. It will give me pleasure to serve you in that or any other Matter,—and I shall assuredly wait the earliest Opportunity to do so—with regard I am,
Dʳ, Sir,
Your most obedient Serv.
Geo: Turner

Major Harleston

RECORDS OF THE REGIMENTS OF THE SOUTH CAROLINA LINE, CONTINENTAL ESTABLISHMENT.

[41.]

[CAPT. THOMAS HALL TO MAJ. ISAAC HARLESTON.]

Addressed: Isaac Harleston Esqr.
    Major of the 2^d Cont^l Reg^t. of S° Carolina
        living at Haddrell's point

                    Tuesday Charles town June 14 1780
D^r. Sir

    M^r. Corbett having no Time to write, requested I would inform you that there was a sufficient quantity of provisions left on y^r places to last your negroes 'till next Crop–your Furniture not abused M^r. Corbett having taken proper care of it—but your liquors were all taken entirely owing to a one Eyed Taylor negro fellow of yours, who went off to the English with his wife, Children & enticed five more—The small pox rages all around your plantation M^r. Corbett has Inoculated his family, he wishes speedily to know your determination with respect to your own Negroes, which he will put in execution immediately—Command me if their is any thing you think I can serve you in
                Y^r. Most Ob^t. Servt.
                    Thomas Hall
I shall go up to Col. Hugers & Capt Shubricks in a few days—if I can procure a horse

[42.]

[RETURN OF THE 1ST. REGIMENT.]

Return of the Officers & Servants of the 1ˢᵗ. Regᵗ. of South Carolina Prisnʳˢ. of war at Haddrell's, Oct. 10ᵗʰ. 1780

		servᵗˢ.
Sick	C. C. Pinckney—Colonel..	Toby a Slave
dº.	Geo. Turner— Captⁿ.....	Isaac Fletcher
	Simeon Theus dº	Thoˢ. Askew
	Joseph Elliott— dº	Bacchus, Slave
dº.	William Hext, dº	Andrew Smith
Sick in Town	Charles Lining dº	Adam Miller
dº.	Thomas Gadsden dº	Jemmy, Slave
	Alexʳ. Fraser Lieutᵗ.....	———————
	John Hamilton dº. & adjutᵗ—	Josʰ: Roberts
Sick in Country	John peter Ward Lᵗ	Hector, Slave
Sick	William Hazzard Lᵗ.	Cain, a Slave
Sick	William Ward dº	Billy a Slave
Sick in Town	Charles Brown dº	Charles dº.
dº.	George Petrie dº.	Tom a Slave
Sick	James Kennedy dº.	Jasper Brownguard

Wᵐ. Russell & James Kenny not in th Line are returned in this Regmᵗ.

G Turner
Captⁿ. 1ˢᵗ. Rᵗ. S. C.

Return of the names of the Officers & Servants of the Sº- Caro line—Prisoners of War in Christ Church Parish Octº- 10ᵗʰ. 1780

54 Total Officers.   43 Servants

[43.]

[RETURN OF THE 3D. REGIMENT.]

Return of the officers & Servants of 3^d- S° Ca^{r}l Reg^t 10th. Oct 1780

	Servts Names
Lt. Col°- Henderson Sick	Neller, slave
Capt. F Warley	Jo^s. D°
Capt. Smith	peter Mgrew soldier
Capt. Jo^s- Warley (sick in Town)	Jas Sword D°
Capt. Goodwyn	Negro Slave
Capt- Buchanan (sick in Town)	Jn° Campbell soldier
Capt Baker	Frances–Slave--
Capt Farrer	Jacob Bruncin Sold^r-
Capt Liddell	———————
Capt pollard	W^m- Myrack D°
Lt Goodwyn	———————
Lt Smith	Jn°- peterkin
L^t MGwire	———————
Doct^r Martin	Jn°- Cauldwell, soldier
Capt Milling late of the 6th. Reg.	W^m- Partridge D°

Merry MGwire Adj^t 3^d- Rg^t

RECORDS OF THE REGIMENTS OF THE SOUTH CAROLINA LINE, CONTINENTAL ESTABLISHMENT.

[44.]

[COL. C. C. PINCKNEY TO MAJ. ISAAC HARLESTON.]

Addressed: Major Harleston [19]

Dear Major,
    I herewith send you a permitt for Lieut^t: Brown to go to Town, and hope he will soon recover his health. I also return you the paper. If there is anything new since yesterday do communicate it. If you have occasion to write home Genl: Moultrie has a servant who will go that way tomorrow & will carry a Letter for you. I forgot to deliver you Miss Moultrie's Compts yesterday and to inquire for her whether you knew how Miss Ashby Harleston did, and whether she had had [break] ll fro [break] I remain
                Yrs sincerely
                Charles Cotesworth Pinckney.

Memorandum on back: Oct^o. 11th: 1780-
    Ordered That each Officer do in Rotation attend to the drawing & distributing of all Rations for the space of one Week beginning wth: Captain Mazyck who will continue to Act 'till Thursday next. The Officers will Order the attendance of their Servants to assist in Conveying the provisions to Barracks as the most Convenient place to be Served out Sickness alone will be an excuse for escaping a Tour—when the next Officer in Succession is to Act

---

[19] The following memorandum is written across the face: "A Ball Bees Wax. Enq$_r$. for Hats— & of whom a Marquis may be borrowed."

[45.]

[A RETURN OF THE 1st REGIMENT.]

Return of the First Regiment of South Carolina Prisoners of War at Haddrell's point, Friday Octr. 1780

	Officers—	White Servants	Blacks
	Col: Ch: C: Pinckney		Toby
	Capt^{ns}. Geo: Turner—	Isaac Fletcher	Boatswain
	Simeon Theus		Bacchus
	Joseph Elliott—	....	....
	William Hext—	Andrew Smith	
	Charles Lining—	Adam Miller	
	Thomas Gadsden—	....	Jemmy
	Lieut^t. Alex^r. Fraser		....
	John Hamilton		Tom
Sick in Count^y.	John P. Ward		Hector
	William Hazzard		Cain
	Charles Brown		Charles
	W^m. Ward		Billy
	Geo: Petrie		Tom
	James Kennedy }		Gasper Brownguard
Not in the Line	William Russell	Peter Dunwick	Wexford
	James Kenny	....	

G. Turner,
Captⁿ 1st. Reg^t. S^o. Carl

Endorsed: 1st. Reg^t.

RECORDS OF THE SOUTH CAROLINA LINE

[46.]

[A RETURN OF THE 2ND REGIMENT.]

Return of the S°. Caro: 2ᵈ. Rgt. prisoners of War at Haddrells point Oct: 20th ·· 1780—

Officers—	White Servants	Blk Servants—
Major Harleston—	Robert Gamble	....
Capts. Mazyck—	....	Toney—
Warley—	....	
Shubrick—	....	Blk boy—Peter.
Baker—	....	
Proveaux—	Sawyer—	....
Mason—	....	Cupid—
Gray—	Ferguson	
Lts—Foissin	Oliver—	
Kolb—	....	York—
Langford	....	
Frierson	....	Julius—
Ogier—	....	....
Evans—	....	Peter—
Legare	Lamb	....
Dunbar	Sparrow	....
Hart—	....	Joe—
Pay Masʳ. Gray	....	Tom—
Lt—Mazyck	....	Robin—

J: Hart Adjt: 2ᵈ. Rgt.

[47.]

[A RETURN OF THE 2ND REGIMENT.]

Return of y̨e So. Car. 2ᵈ. Rgt. prisoners of War at Haddrells point—Oct. 28ᵗʰ. 1780—

Officers—	White Servants	Black Servants
Major Harleston	Robert Gamble	
Capts. Mazyck	....	Peter
Warley	....	....
Shubrick	....	Peter
Baker	....	....
Proveaux	....	....
Mason	....	Cupid
Gray	Ferguson	
Lts. Foissin	Thoˢ. Oliver	
Kolb	....	York
Langford	....	....
Frierson	....	Julius
In Town Ogier	....	....
Evans	....	Peter
Legare	Lamb	....
Dunbar	Jnº Sparrow	
Hart	....	Joe
Mazyck	....	Robin
Pay Mas= Gray	....	Tom

[48]

[A Return of the 3rd Regiment.]

Return of the Officers & Servants of the 3ᵈ Sᵒ. Cʳ. Regt Now Prisoners of War at Hadrills Point 29 Octʳ. 1780—

Lt. Colᵒ. Henderson	....	Nelson a Slave
Capᵗ. F. Warley	Sick in Town	
Capᵗ. Smith	....	Peter MGrew soldier
Capᵗ. Joˢ. Warley	present	Jaˢ.Swords Dᵒ Taylor
Capᵗ. Goodwyn	....	
Capᵗ. Buchanan	Sick in Town	Jnᵒ. Campbell soldier
Capᵗ. Baker	....	....
Capᵗ. Farrer	....	Jacob Bruncin Sol
Capᵗ. Liddell	....	....
Capᵗ. Pollard	....	Wᵐ. Myrack Dᵒ
Lᵗ. Goodwyn	....	Wᵐ. Partridge
Lᵗ. Smith	....	Jnᵒ. Peterkin
Lᵗ. MGwire	....	Joˢ. Williams
Lᵗ. Capᵗ. Milling	....	....
Doctʳ. Martin	....	Cauldwell soldier

Merry MGwire Adgᵗ. 3ᵈ Regᵗ
Jnᵒ. C: Smith Capt.

[49.]

[A Return of the 1st Regiment.]

Return of the Officers & Servants of the first Regim^t. of So. Caro: Novr. 10th /80

	Col: C C. Pinckney	Toby a Negro
	Captn. Geo: Turner	Isaac Fletcher
	Simeon Theus—	Boatswain, a Negro
	Joseph Elliott—	Bacchus—— d^o.
	W^m. Hext—	Andrew Smith
	Charles Lining—	Adam Miller
Sick in T.	Thomas Gadsden—	Jemmy a Negro
D^o.	Lieut^t. Alex^r. Fraser	……… ……… ………
	John Hamilton	Tom a Negro
Sick in Co^y.	John P. Ward	Hector d^o.
	W^m. Hazzard	Cain d^o.
D^o. Town.	Charles Brown	Charles d^o.
	William Ward	Billy d^o.
D^o. in Town.	George petrie	Tom d^o.
	James Kennedy	Gasp: Brownguard
Not in ye line	{ W^m. Russell	peter Dunwick
	{ James Kenny	Wexford a Negro
	G Turner	
	Captn 1st. Reg^t So Car:	

Endorsed: Return
1st. Reg^t.

RECORDS OF THE SOUTH CAROLINA LINE 65

[50.]

[A RETURN OF THE 1ST REGIMENT.]

Weekly Return of the 1st. Regt. of So. Carolina at Haddrell's —— November 1780

Officers	Servants	Remarks
Col: Charles C. Pinckney	Toby (Slave)—	
Captains Geo: Turner	Isaac Fletcher	
Simeon Theus	Boatswain (Slave)	
Joseph Elliott	Bacchus (d°)	
William Hext	Andrew Smith	
Charles Lining	Adam Miller	
Thomas Gadsden	Jemmy (Slave)	Sick in Town
Lieut'. Alexander Fraser	....	D°.
John Hamilton	Tom (d°.)	
John Peter Ward	Hector (d°.)	Sick Country
Wm. Hazzard	Cain (d°.)	
Charles Brown	Charles (d°.)	D°. Town
William Ward	Billy (d°.)	Sick Barracks
George Petrie	Tom (d°.)	D°. Town
James Kennedy	Gaspar Brownguard	D°. Barracks
James Kenny	Wexford (Slave)	⎧ Not in the line
Wm. Russell	Peter Dunwick	⎨ but returned
		⎩ in this Regimt

G Turner
Captn 1st. Rt.

[51.]

[A MUTILATED RETURN OF THE 1ST REGIMENT.]

	Elliott	Bacchus d°.
	Hext	And*. Smith
	Lining	Adam Miller
Sick in Town	Gadsden	Jemmy, Negro
	Lieu^{ts}. Fraser	....
	Hamilton	Tom, Negro
d°. Count^y.	J. P. Ward	Hector, d°.
	Hazzard	Cain— d°.
Sick in Town	Charl. Brown	Charles d°.
	W^m. Ward	Billy d°.
Sick Town	George petrie	Tom
	Kennedy	G. Brownguard
Not in ye Line	{ W^m. Russell	P. Dunwick
	{ Ja^s. Kenny	Wexford—
		G Turner
		Captⁿ 1st. R^t. So. Caro.

Subs. 4 absent
Capt^s. 1.........4 slaves absent
Endorsed: Return Say November 25th 1780

Waiters { Present

{ Absent

[52.]

[LIEUTENANT GEORGE EVANS TO MAJOR ISAAC HARLESTON.]

Addressed: Major Harleston
2^d. S. C. Reg^t.

Lieut. Evanss Compliments wait on Major Harleston beg the favor of his permission to go to Town L^t. Evans's Name has been upon the list at General Moultrie's ever since August and has been waiting patiently since for leave but have not been able to procure leave the Certificate will shew my situation which L^t. E. beg the Major to take notice of—

RECORDS OF THE REGIMENTS OF THE SOUTH CAROLINA LINE, CONTINENTAL ESTABLISHMENT.

[53.]

[REV. ROBERT SMITH TO MAJOR ISAAC HARLESTON.]

Addressed: Maj^r. Harleston—
of the 2^d. Sth Carolina

Dear Sir—

Some days past, I dined in Company with Lieut: Makerill of the 64th—who inform'd me, he had sent a Message to a Maj^r. Harleston, about a Negro of his, whom he was ready to deliver. I immediately let him know, that this s^d. Maj^r. Harleston was an acquaintance, & with his permission I would write to you—His answer was, yes—but added, that on not hearing from you, he had let an Officer of the same Regiment have the Fellow, not having use for him himself—that the Gentleman's name was Warner—on which another Officer observed to me that it was the very Gentleman, who was quartered on me (or rather Tom Grimball, at whose house I now am)—on going home, I called the Fellow (whose name is Ballifo) & ask'd to whom he belong'd—he s^d to you—& that he was forc'd away from the Plantation by M^r. Mackerill to look after Horses—that he had frequently requested to go home—& that Mr Warner had told him he should go home very soon—please to observe that Mackerill told me, he took the Fellow from the Plantation, & that he believes Ballifo w^d. not have come away *of himself.*—Ballifo told me that a Sorrell Colt with a blaz'd face, was at M^r. Manigaults opposite to Grimballs—which was your Colt—on enquiring, I saw it—and found it was taken by a Captn Crane of the 33^d.—quartered at Manigaults, but who was gone to York, & had given his Horses to his Servant—& that y^r. price for the Colt was *five Guineas*—a large sum this—but which on your account I w^d. have given—but alass—I am *Guinealess*— —not a shilling—much more a Guinea— —I believe the Colt is now sold, not having seen him some time. —Warner is march'd on detachment to Monks Corner, with Provisions, & took Ballifo with him—who perhaps may elope, and save further trouble—Adieu may health attend you—with her hand-maid happiness—

      Y^{rs}.. truly
       Robt Smith
        Thursday—

[54.]

[A RETURN OF THE 1ST. REGIMENT.]

Weekly Return of the 1st. Reg^t. of South Carolina Pris^n of War at Haddrell's Point Novr 10th. | 80

	Officers	Serv^{ts}.
	Col. C. C. Pinckney	Toby a Negro
	Captn. Geo: Turner—	Isaac Fletcher
	Simeon Theus—	Boatswain
	Joseph Elliott—	Bacchus, a Negro
Sick	W^m. Hext—	Andrew Smith
	Charles Lining—	Adam Miller
Sick in Town	Thomas Gadsden—	Jemmy, a Negro
d^o.	Lieut: Alex^r. Fraser—	
	John Hamilton—	Tom a Negro
Sick in Country	John P- Ward—	Hector d^o—
	W^m. Hazzard—	Cain d^o—
d^o.	Town Charles Brown—	Charles d^o.
	W^m. Ward—	Billy d^o-
D^o	George Petrie—	Tom d^o.
	James Kennedy—	G. Brownguard
	Wm Russell } not in the Line	Peter Dunwick
	Ja^s. Kenny }	Wexford, Negro

      G. Turner
      Captn 1st. Reg^t. So. Caro:

[55]
[A RETURN OF THE 1ST. REGIMENT.]

Addressed: Major Harleston

Return of the Officers of the 1st. Regt. S. C.
who have lost Servants by Death &
Desertion—with the names of such
Servants opposed—   Novr. 12th. 1780

   Captn. Geo: Turner...John Fleming, deserted
   Simeon Theus......... Askew, do.
Inlisted with ⎱ Joseph Elliott......... Benjn. Teaster, do.
the British[20] ⎰ Thos. Gadsden........ Zekiel Malpas do.
   Lieut. Jno. Hamilton......... Joseph Roberts,— do.
   Wm. Hazzard.......... Never had a Servt.
   John P. Ward......... Absolam Hooper, desertd
Davis— ⎱
Deserted ⎰ Charles Brown... Never had a Servt.
   William Ward... Lemon, deserted
   George Petrie ⎰ Cherry, taken up
        ⎱ & returned as a
         British Deserter
      G Turner Captn 1st. Rt. S. C

G Turner returns his Complimts. to Major Harleston—sends him in compliance with the Major's Note the Return required—being the first application of the kind received
            Sunday Noon
Memorandum on back: G. Warley Decr. 26. 1777
    D Langford

---

[20] This, of course, does not mean that Captains Elliott and Gadsden so enlisted but that their deserters did.

[56.]

[A RETURN OF THE 3RD. REGIMENT.]

Return of the 3ᵈ Sᵒ. Carˡ. Regᵗ prisoners of War at Hadˡˢ. point 24 Novʳ 1780

	Officers	Servants Names
	Lt Colo. Wᵐ. Henderson	Kneller A Slave
Sick in Town {	Capt Felix Warley	Joˢ. a Slave
	Capt Jnᵒ. C. Smith	Peter MGrew
	Capt. Joˢ. Warley	Jaˢ. Sword Taylor
	Capt U. Goodwyn	A Negroe Slave
Sick in Town {	Capt Jnᵒ. Buchanan	Jnᵒ. Campbell
	Capt Jesse Baker	Frances a Slave
	Capt Field Farrer	Jacob Bruncin
	Capt Geᵒ Liddell	
	Capt Richᵈ Pollard	Wᵐ: Myrack
	Lieut Jnᵒ Goodwyn	Wᵐ Partridge
	Ltⁿ Aaron Smith	Jno Peterkin
	Ltⁿ Merry MGuire	Joˢ Williams
Doᶜʳ	Jaˢ Martin	Jnᵒ Cauldwell
	Merry MGuire Agt 3ᵈ Regt	

Endorsed: 3ᵈ Sᵒ Carˡ.

Memoranda:

Felix Warley	James Hayes, deserted	
Jo Warley	Joseph Haynes	dᵒ–
Goodwyn	Wᵐ= Chapman	dᵒ
Baker	James White	dᵒ
Liddell	Benjˢ. Culpepper	dᵒ–
Lᵗ. Goodwyn	Samˡ. Kelly	dᵒ–
Smith	James Wilson	d –
Mᶜ= Guire	Elijah McGuire	dᵒ–

[57.]

[A RETURN OF THE 1ST. REGIMENT.]

Return of the 1st. Regt. So. Caro: prisoners at Haddrell's, Friday 6.[21] 1780

			servts.
sick	Col: C. C.	Pinckney	Toby, Negro
	Captns.	Turner	Isaac Fletcher
		Theus	Boatswain, Negro
		Elliott	Bacchus——do.
		Hext	Andr. Smith
		Lining	Adam Miller
Do.		Gadsden	January, a Negro
Do. Lieutt.		Fraser	
		Hamilton	Tom a Negro
Do. Country		J. P. Ward	Hector do.
		Hazzard	Cain do.
		Brown	Charles do.
		W. Ward	Billy do.
		Petrie	Tom do.
		Kennedy	G. Brownguard

Wm. Russell & Servant no longer to be returned——

G Turner
Captn 1st Rt. So. C

---

[21] December is evidently the missing month.

[58.]

[A RETURN OF THE 3RD. REGIMENT.]

Weekly Return of the 3ᵈ Sº. Carˡ. regᵗ. at Haddrell's point 22ᵈ Decʳ 1780

Officers Names	Servᵗˢ. Names
Lt Colº. Wᵐ. Henderson	Kneller a Slave
Capt F. Warley	Joˢ. a Slave
Capt Jnº. C. Smith	Peter McGraw
Capt Joˢ. Warley	…………………………
Capt U. Goodwyn	Harry a Slave
Capt Jnº. Buchanan	Jnº. Campbell
Capt Jesse Baker	Will a Slave
Capt F Farrer	Jacob Bruncin
Capt Geº Liddell	…………………………
Capt Richᵈ Pollard	Wᵐ- Myrack
Lieut. Jnº Goodwyn	Wᵐ. Partridge
Lt Arin Smith	Jnº Peterkin
Lt Merry M Guire	Joˢ Williams
Dʳ Jaˢ. Martin	Jnº Cauldwell
	James Sword Taylor
	Merry M Guire
	for 3ᵈ Regᵗ

[59.]

[A RETURN OF THE 1ST. REGIMENT.]

Return of Servants of 1st. Regt. of So: Caro:—dead, deserted, Sick in Hospital and present—with the Name of each officer whom they serve set opposite Haddrell's Jany 7th. 1781

Dead	Deserted	Sick in Hosp'.	Present	Officers
	Sergt. Oats		None	Col: C. C. Pinckney
	Absoms. Hooper		Isaac Fletcher	Capts. Turner
	Thos. Askew		None	........Theus
	Teaster		None	........Elliott
			Andrew Smith	........Hext
	Robt. Black		Adam Miller	........Lining
	Zekiel Malpas		None	........Gadsden
			None	Lieuts. Fraser
	Joseph Roberts		None	........Hamilton
	James Lemon		None	........J. P. Ward
			None	........Hazzard
	Edmd. Davis		None	........Brown
	John Nelson		None	........W. Ward
			None	........*Petrie
			Gaspar Brownguard	........Kennedy

*Lt. Petrie's servt being a Deserter from the British was ⎫ G Turner
claimed & taken back by them   ⎬ Captn. 1st.Regt. So: Caro:

RECORDS OF THE REGIMENTS OF THE SOUTH CAROLINA LINE, CONTINENTAL ESTABLISHMENT.

[60.]

[A RETURN OF THE 3D. REGIMENT.]

Addressed: Major Harleston
2^d: reg^t..S° C^a-

Return of the Officers & Serv^{ts}.. of the Second S°.. Carolina reg^t.—

Maj^{or} Harleston	white	Robt.. Gambell
Captn.. Mazyck	blk	Peter
Captn.. Warley	— — — — — — —	
Captn Shubrick	blk	Peter
Captn.. Baker		
Captn.. Provaux		
Captn.. Mason		
Captn.. Gray	white	Ferguson
Lieut^t.. Foissin	do..	Tom: Oliver
Lt Kolb	blk	York
L^t.. Langford		
L^t.. Frierson	do..	Julius
L^t.. Ogier		
L^t.. Evans	blk	Peter
Lt Legare	white	Lamb
Lt Dunbar	d°	Jn° Sparrow
Lt Hart		
Lt.. Mazyck	blk	Robin
Pay Master Gray	D°	Tom

[61.]
[A GUARD DETAIL OF THE 2D. REGIMENT.]

	On duty	Fit for duty	Guard—
Mazyck	3	4	2
Warley	3	6	3
Shubrick	1	2	1
Baker	1	2	1
Proveaux	1	3	2
Mason	2	2	1
Gray	1	—	0
Vacant	2	5	2
			12

Guard Sergt: Roberts
Corp¹—Lions

Capt Mazyck   Maz⁷
   Warley
   Shubrick   Shubrick
   Baker
   Provaux   Provaux
   Mason   Gray
   Gray

   Colonels   Wacant
                     Mason
                     Baker
                     Warley

[62.]

[A RETURN OF THE 2D. REGIMENT.]

Return of the S°.. Caro: 2ᵈ Rgt: prisoners of war at Haddrells

Major Harleston......Robert Gamble
  Capt.. Mazyck..................................Toney
       Warley..
       Shubrick...Peter
       Baker..Joe
       Proveaux..Harry
in Town Mason..
       Gray............................Ferguson......
Lts.. Martin..................................
       Foissin....................Oliver......
       Kolb......................................
       Langford.................................
       Frierson......................Julius
       Ogier.....................................
       Evans...................................Peter
       Legare........................Lamb............
       Dunbar........................Sparrow.........
       Hart......................................
       Mazyck.............................Robin
Pay Masʳ: Gray...Tom—

On Back: Be the Hearts blood spilled that does the Act. the tongue accursed that durst avow the purpose, & the Hand blasted that obeys the Order

[63.]

[A RETURN OF THE 3D. REGIMENT.]

Return of the 3ᵈ S Carˡ Regᵗ Prisoners of War at Hadrells Point 20 Jan. 1781————————————

Lt Colo. Henderson	....	Kneller a Slave
Captains, F. Warley	....	Joˢ.. a Slave
Smith	....	Peter MGrew
Joˢ. Warley	....	
Goodwyn	....	Peter a Slave
in the country Buchanan	....	Jnº. Campbell
Town Baker	....	Will a Slave
Farrer	....	Jacob Bruucin
Liddell	....	
Pollard	....	Willm. Myrack
Lieuts— Goodwyn	....	Wm. Partridge
Smith	....	Jnº Peterkin
MGwire	....	Joˢ Williams
Docʳ Martin		Jnº Caldwell
		James Sword Taylor
		Merry MGwire
		Adjt. 3ᵈ Regt

[64.]

[SEGOUD TO MAJOR ISAAC HARLESTON.]

Addressed: Major Harleston*
of the South Carolina line

8 march 1781

Sir
having been inform'd by mr. edwar [a letter or two gone] that the pay of the legionary officers had been left into your hands—I desir'd the lieut. 20th to wait upon you to receive it and bring it to me who as the eldest officer of the corps am better acquaint'd with their circumstances and will pay them off to their satisfaction undouptely you got our pay roll and know the capts have the majors of infantry's pay 50^{dollars} the lieu^t. 33^d-⅔ and the cornet—26^d-⅓
I heard that the Staff was to be pay'd their extra; and in consequence of it the officers of the lines was not not to be pay'd till that money comes but as there is no such instance in the remanes of the corps I think that if the money of ours is in your hands the desire of our officers is to receive it sooner than latter some of them tho the sum small being still in want of it.
undouptely the money coming to the prisoners of the 16th of august now present on hadrills-point, and belonging to the legion is in your hand; if so as they are in the same quarter and of the same opinion they hope you'll be pleas'd to convey their money by the lieut. roth—
        I am Sir
             with respect
                your most obed
                   Segoud/:

---

* "Henderson" was stricken out and "Harleston" inserted after "Major".

[65.]

[MRS. ELIZABETH HARTH TO MAJOR ISAAC HARLESTON.]

Addressed: To
  Capt". Isaac Harlston
    Hadrels point

Charles Town May 30: 1781—
The Schoolmaster and the Doctor that attended Miss Agnus Parkerson Calls on me and threatens to sue me for Payment, and as you were to kind as to tell me you would see that Paid, & Likewise her Boarding, I thought Proper to acquaint you of it first, in hope you will let me know by a few Lines, who I am to Call upon for Payment, as it is to be paid—immediately   I am with Great esteem

Y^r. Obd^t. hble Servant
Elizabeth Harth
formerly E: Holson

Capt". Harlston

INDEX

-A-

Adair (Lt) 32
Adams, Andrew 2, 3, 4
  Ezekiel 11, 12
Adkins (Bartley, Bart.) 23
Albert (William, Wm.) 2, 4
Allison, Joseph 21
Ammonds/Amonds, Joshua 20
Anderson, Abraham 49
  Isaac 14
  Samuel 26
  Thomas 18
  (William, Wm.) 14
Andy (Chrisr., Christr.) 19
Anthony, Charles 22
Archart, John 20
Ashbury, James 18
Askew,_____ 69
  Thos. 57, 73
Astlow,_____ 4
Atkinson, John 22

-B-

Baillie, Robert C. 18
Baker,_____ 53, 70
  (Capt) 3, 32, 33, 46, 47, 48, 50, 58, 61, 62, 63, 74-77
  (Lt) 5
  J. 54
  Jesse 34, 70, 72
  Richard Bohun 34
  Richd. 43
Balium, Icabod 23
Ballifo,_____ 67, 68
Banks, James 14
Barker (Thomas, Thos.) 20
Barnett, John 14
Batheny,_____ 4
Bean, James 14
  (William, Wm.) 14
Beaseley/Beasley, Peter 23
Berry, Charles 15
Bill, Samuel 21
Binam/Bynum (Benjamin, Ben) 15

Bird, Robert 14
Bishop, Wm. 35
Black, James 14
  Robt. 73
Blackley/Blakley (Bland, Blan) 17
Blair/Blare, Wade 24
Blake (Capt) 2, 3
Bone, John 17
Bonett (Sarg) 4
Boon, Isaac 15
Booth/Boothe, John 16
Bowen, John 20
Bowers, Randolph 22
Bowland, James 22
Boyes (Capt) 12, 32
Bradwell (Lt) 33, 34
Brazell/Brazil, Jacob 17
Bremar, Francis 7
Brett, Richard 22
Breyler, Jacob 2, 3
Bridgewater, Elias 22
  Isaac 22
Broadaway, Edward 19
Brooks, Joseph 15
Brooner, William 9
Brown,_____ 4, 7
  (Capt) 33
  (Lt) 32, 33, 59, 71, 73
Bozwell 23
  (Charles, Charl.) 57, 60, 64-66, 68, 69
  Jno. 10
  Stephen 24
  (Will, Wm.) 3, 19
Brownguard, G. 66, 68, 71
  (Gasper, Gasp., Jasper) 57, 60, 64, 65, 73
Bruce, Moses 3, 4
Bruncin/Brunsin (Jacob, Jacb.) 54, 58, 63, 70, 72, 77
Brunson/Brunston, Jacob 24
Brushears (Samuel, Saml.) 25
Bryan, William 26
Brynson (George, Geo.) 2, 3, 4
Buchanan,_____ 32
  (Capt) 33, 34, 58, 63, 77
  (Lt) 33, 34

Buchanan (cont)
  J. 54
  Jno. 70; 72
Buchannan (Capt) 12
Bulls (Gen) 10
Bunch, John 16
Burges, James 23
Burkett (Thomas, Thos.) 2, 3
Burns, Thomas 18
Bussby/Brozbe, Jesse 23
Bussby/Busby, John 26
Butler, Joseph 11
Byrd, Robert 14

-C-

Caddy, Jno. 4
Cain (Michael, Michl.) 22
Caldwell, John 22
  William 21, 28, 30
Camble (Ezekial, Ezekiel) 16
  Isom 20
Camble/Campbell (Robert, Robt.) 18
Campbell, Jno. 54, 58, 63, 70, 72, 77
  Saml. 17
Cample, John 16
Canaday (William, Wm.) 20
Cantley, James 16
Capers,_____ 53
  (Lt) 46
  William 43
Carey, Isaac 25
Carless/Carloss, Wm. 18
Carmichael, Richard 24
Carter, Benjn. 17
  Geo. 17
  James 24, 26
Cates, George 15
Cauldwell,_____ 63
Cauldwell/Caldwell, Jno. 54, 58, 70, 72, 77
Caves, Jno. 4
Chancey, Edmund 22
Chapman (William, Wm.) 19, 20, 54, 70
Charnock, C. 3
Chavers, Elisha 15
Chavis, John 24
  William 24

Cherry, _____ 69
Clark/Clarke, John 19
Clay, Joseph 28, 30
Clements, Thomas 21
Clyatt, _____ 4
Cobia, Francis 45
Cochrin (Corp) 11
Collier, Isaac 24
Collins, _____ 4
Colman (Robert, Robt.) 2, 3
Connell, _____ 4
Connors, Nathaniel 15
Cook, John 26
  Wm. 4
Copeland, Reuben 22
Copland, J. 3
  Jacob 2
Corbett (Mr) 37, 56
Coronat (Capt) 52
Cosang, Jon. 11
Covington, Henry 21
Coudene/Cowden, John 23
Crane (Capt) 67
  Will. 17
Crawford, John 9
  Thomas 9
Crim/Crimm, Wm. 19
Croft, Samuel 24
Cross, Samuel 23
Crouther, Isaac 6
Crowley, Croker 20
Crowther, Jesse 24
Crum, Henry 22
Culpepper (Benjamin, Benja.) 25, 70
Cumbee, J. Jordan 3

-D-

Davice (Mr) 45
Davis, _____ 37, 69
  Edmd. 73
  (Jeremiah, Jeremh.) 26
  Jno. 35
  William 23
Dean/Deen, John 17
  (Thomas, Tho.) 17
DeBrahm (Maj) 36, 40, 141
deCamp, A. 51
Declandenease/Declen-denese, Mathew 20
DeSaussure (Lt) 6
  D. 14, 29
  (Lewis, Louis) 14, 29
Devis/Devors, Charles 15
Dewley, Robert 14
Disto, Moses 22
Dodd, _____ 10
Doggett (Capt) 11, 32
  (Lt) 32
  Rd. 12
Dogharty/Dogherty, James 24
Douglas, Thos. 54
Douglas/Douglass, Thomas 26
Douglass/Dougles, James 23
Downer, Moses 18
Downing (Timothy, Timy., Tim.) 2, 3, 4
Doyer/Dyer, John 26
Doyley (Lt) 33

Draper, James 26
Drayton (Capt) 10
Driver, Henry 20
Dunbar, _____ 47, 48, 50, 53
  (Capt) 46
  (Lt) 61, 62, 74, 76
Dunlap, Robert 23
Dunwick, P. 66
  Peter 60, 64, 65, 68
Dupont, Josiah 45

-E-

Edens, John 24
Edwar (Mr) 78
Edwards, William 21
Eggerton, James 24
Elkins (Johnson, Johnston) 19
Ellidge, William 23
Elliott, _____ 66
  (Capt) 10, 33, 34, 71, 73
  Joseph 57, 60, 64, 65, 68, 69
Ellis, Edward 24
Evance (Lt) 46
Evanes, _____ 47
Evans, _____ 48, 50, 53
  (Lt) 34, 61, 62, 74, 76
  Abram 18
  Benjamin 22
  (George, Geo.) 43, 44, 66

-F-

Fagen, Peter 2-4
Falkner, Edward 20
Farrar, Field 23-25, 28, 30
  Jesse 17
Farrer (Capt) 58, 63, 77
  F. 54, 72
  Field 70
Fatherree (Benjamin, Benja.) 21
Fenicke, _____ 4
Fenner, Lucetta E. 14
Fenwicke (John, Jno.) 2-4
Ferguson, _____ 61, 62, 74, 76
Finney, James 19
  John 18
  Michael 18
Fishburn (Capt) 33
Fitzpatrick (Lt) 6
Fleming, John 17, 69
Fletcher, Isaac 57, 60, 64, 65, 68, 71, 73
  William 5
Flick, John 24
Florida, Morris 21
Foissin, _____ 47, 48, 50, 53
  (Lt) 46, 61, 62, 74, 76
Fossine, Peter 43
Foster, Henry 26
Fowler, Maurice 15
Foxworth, Samuel 25

Franklin, Easum 17
Frankum, Francis 24
Fraser (Lt) 34, 35, 36, 66, 71, 73
  (Alexander, Alexr.) 57, 60, 64, 65, 68
Frazer (1 Lt) 10
Freeman (James, Jas.) 2, 3
  Joseph 26
Frierson, _____ 47, 48, 50
  (Lt) 61, 62, 74, 76
  John 43, 44
Fulk, Henry 27
Fulker, John 22
Fulmer, John 17

-G-

Gadsden, _____ 66
  (Capt) 10, 33, 71, 73
  (Thomas, Thos.) 57, 60, 64, 65, 68, 69
Galaspie, James 17
Gamble/Gambell (Robert, Robt.) 61, 62, 74, 76
Gassett, Isaac 18
Gaston, Robert 26
Gibbes, _____ 7
Gibson, _____ 4
  Daniel 24
  Robert 15
Gicken, John 15
Gill (Thomas, Thos.) 22
Gillen/Gillon, John 15
Ginkins, James 20
Goar, Saml. 16
Godfrey (William, Wm.) 22
Goodin (Richard, Richd.) 2, 3
Goodwin (Capt) 9
  Richd. 4
Goodwyn, _____ 70
  (Capt) 34, 58, 63, 77
  (Lt) 58, 63, 70, 77
  Britton 26
  J. 54
  (John, Jno.) 19, 29, 70, 72
  U. 54, 70, 72
Goodwyn/Gooden, Miles 23
Goodwyn/Goodwin, Uriah 6, 19, 20, 28, 30
Gordon (Benjamin, Benjn.) 20
Gore (Ashford, Ash) 17
Gosling/Gossling, George 21
Gough, James 16
Gousmald, Henry 16
Gray, _____ 47, 53, 61, 62, 74, 76
  (Capt) 34, 42, 43, 47, 48, 50, 61, 62, 74-76
  Henry 43
  Peter 43
Green, _____ 4
  Daniel 2-4
  Paul 26
Griffen/Griffin, Gideon 25
Griffin, Morgan 25
Griggoray/Grigory, Henry 27
Grimball, Tom 67

Grimke (Lt Col) 51, 52
Grimkee (Col) 53
Groomes, Gilbert 24
Gruver (Sarg) 11

-H-

Hackles, Fred 16
Haddocks, Isaac 16
Hagarthy,_____ 4
Haig, John James 28, 29
Hall (Capt) 46
  George Abbott 37
  (Thomas, Thos.) 43, 56
Hamilton (Lt) 66, 71, 73
  (John, Jno.) 57, 60,
  64, 65, 68, 69
Hamlet/Hamlett, Carter 17
Hampton (Capt) 32, 33
Hamton (Capt) 11
Hanson (William, Wm.) 2-4
Hanson/Hinson, William 22
Hardaway, Joel 17
Hardick, Wm. 15
Harleston (Maj) 11, 12,
  34, 37, 38, 40, 41,
  44, 47, 49, 51-53,
  55, 61, 62, 69, 74,
  76
  Ashby 59
  I. 12, 13
  Isaac 7, 30, 36-38, 45,
  56, 59, 66, 67, 78,
  79
Harper, Josiah 27
  Wilkins 20
  Wm. 3
Harris, Dreury 25
  Peter 23
  (Thomas, Thos.) 16
Harrison, George 25
Hart,_____ 47, 48,
  50, 53
  (Lt) 46, 61, 62, 74,
  76
  George 24
  J. 61
Harth, Elizabeth 79
Harvey, Bakie 22
Haskins/Hasskin, John 20
Haslam (William, Wm.) 14
Hayes, James 70
  John 21
Haynes (Joseph, Jos.) 19,
  54, 70
Haze, James 18
  John 18
Hazzard (William, Wm.)
  57, 60, 64, 65, 68,
  69
Hazzard/Hazard (Lt) 33,
  66, 71, 73
Hellary, John 17
Henderson,_____ 78
  (Col) 3
  (Lt Col) 9, 36, 38, 52,
  58, 63, 77
  (William, Wm.) 45, 70,
  72
Henington/Heninton, John
  26-28 30
Henson (Will., Wm.) 18
Henson/Hinson, Jesse 27
Herindine, Thos. 17
Heron (Frederick, Fredk.)
  24

Hext,_____ 66
  (Capt) 33, 71, 73
  (William, Wm.) 57, 60,
  64, 65, 68
Hill, Daniel 21
Hinds, A. 3
  Anthony 2
  (John, Jno.) 2, 3
Hines, Robert 11
Hogg, James 23
Hogwood, Henry 17
Holley (Benjamin, Benj.)
  25
Holloway, Taylor 26
Holson, E. 79
Hood, Nathaniel 22
  Robert 21
Hooper (Absolam, Absom.)
  69, 73
Hope, George 16
Hopkins,_____ 29
  D. 6
  David 16, 28, 30
Horn (Samuel, Saml.) 2-4
Horne,_____ 4
Horner (Thomas, Thos.) 15
Horry (Lt Col) 38
Houselighter, Michael 15
Howe (Gen) 10
Howell, Francis 21
Huger (Col) 56
Hughes, Edward 23
Humphreys, John 16
Hunt, John 22
Hunter, John 16
Hutson (Samuel, Saml.) 27
Hutto, Henry 22
Hyrne (Capt) 10
  (Maj) 37, 38

-I-

Inlow, John 16
Isaacs, John 27

-J-

Jackson (Ambrose, Ambros)
  25
  (John, Jno.) 2, 3, 15
  Miles 23
James, Joseph 27
  William 25
Jeffers (Allan, Allen)
  25
  Berry 25
  Osborn 25
Jenkins, Wm. 3
Jinkens, Reason 19
Jnoston., Fredk. 3
John, Ezael 15
Johnson, Abraham 27
  (Benjamin, Benjn.) 21
  Frederick 2
  (William, Wm.) 21
Johnson/Johnston,
  Elijah 26
  (Mathew, Matthew) 25
Johnston (Sarg) 13
  Britton 23
  James 20
  (Robert, Robt.) 14, 29

Jones, Elijah 19
  James 23
  John 21, 27
  R. 6
  Raymond 23
  Richd. 17
  Tho. 35
  (Will, Wm.) 19
  (William, Wm.) 19
  Wm. P. 3
  Wm. Skipper 2
Joyner, Joseph 15
Julian, Andrew 23

-K-

Kearsey/Kersey, Philip 24
Keenan/Keenenen, James 25
Keller, Henry 17
Kelly/Kelley, Saml. 18,
  54, 70
Kembler, Henry 22
Kenaday/Kennaday, Robt.
  16
Kennedy (Lt) 33, 66, 71,
  73
  James 57, 60, 64, 65,
  68
  William 7
Kenny (James, Jas.) 57,
  60, 64-66, 68
Killgore, Henry 21
  James 21
King, John 15
Kirkpatrick, James 15
Klendall, Luke 3
Knap/Knapp, John 22
Knighton (William, Wm.)
  27
Knolton, G. 3
Kolb,_____ 47, 48, 50,
  53
  (Lt) 43, 46, 61, 62,
  74, 76
  Josiah 2, 3, 43

-L-

Lamb,_____ 4, 61, 62,
  74, 76
Lampley, Thos. 3
Lane (Benjamin, Benj.) 27
  Edward 26
  Langford,_____ 47, 48,
  50
  (Lt) 32-34, 61, 62, 74,
  76
  D. 69
  Danl. 43, 44
Lappin, Peter 49
Lassiter, Thadius 15
Laumoy (Col) 36
Laurance/Lawrence, John
  18
Lauson, Anthony 27
Lawton, Winborn Wallace
  (Mrs) 14
Lee, John 18
Lefever, John, 21
LeFevre, Jno. 3
Legare,_____ 47, 48,
  50, 53

83

Legare (cont)
  James 43
Legare/Lagare/Legire (Lt)
  43, 46, 49, 61, 62,
  74, 76
Lemon, _____ 69
  James 73
Lesesne (Capt) 3
Levachar (Lt) 10
Levacher (Capt) 33
Leviston/Livingston,
  Moses 23
Lewis, Benjamin 19
Liddell, _____ 70
  (Capt) 58, 63, 77
  G. 54
  (George, Geo.) 25, 26,
  28, 30, 70, 72
Lincoln (Gen) 1, 37, 53
  (Lt) 44
Lining, _____ 66
  (Capt) 33, 71, 73
  Charles 57, 60, 64,
  65, 68
Linning (Capt) 10
Lions (Corp) 75
Lipencott, Jonathan 16
Looft, John 23
Love (William, Wm.) 19,
  54
Loveman/Lovemon, John 16
Lyons, Jno. 3, 4
Lytle (Lt) 9

-M-

Mace, _____ 4
Mackerill/Makerill (Mr)
  67
Madcap, Squire 18
Main, John 21
Malpas, Zekiel 69, 73
Manigault (Mr) 67
Marion (Col) 43, 46, 53
  (Lt Col) 36, 38, 43
  Francis 42, 43
Markey, _____ 4
Marques/Marquise, Joseph
  11, 12
Martin, _____ 50, 53
  (Capt) 46
  (Dr) 58, 63, 77
  (Lt) 43, 76
  Adam 14
  (James, Jam., Jas.)
  (Dr) 28, 29, 54, 70,
  72
  John 15, 43
  Martin 23
  Richard 35
Mason, _____ 53
  (Capt) 34, 42, 43, 46,
  47, 48, 50, 61, 62,
  74, 75, 76
  Richard 7, 43
Massey, William 44
Mathews, _____ 30
Matts, John M. 17
Matts/Mats, Michael 20
Mayson (Lt Col) 6
  James 28, 29
  Luke 16
Mazyck, _____ 47, 48, 50
  (Capt) 34, 42, 43, 46-
  48, 50, 53, 59, 61,
  62, 74-76

Mazyck (cont)
  (Lt) 34, 61, 62, 74, 76
  Daniel 43
McCabe, Patrick 22
McCafferty, John 20
McCartey, Alexander 20
McCarty, Dennis 19
McCaseel/McCaskill
  (Findlay, Finlay) 16
McCloud, Tartle 14
McCollough/McCullough,
  Hugh 15
McCormack, Charles 19
McCullogh, Wm. 2, 3
McCune, John 20
McDaniell/Mcdenniel,
  James 25
McDowall (Thomas, Thos.)
  22
McElwee, James 15
McGee, John 16
McGraw (Arthur, Arther)
  19
McGraw/MGrew, Peter 16,
  54, 58, 63, 70, 72,
  77
McGraws, Solomon 22
McGrew, Peter 25
McGuire, Alexr. 19
McGuire/Mguire (Elijah,
  Elijh.) 20, 54, 70
McGuire/MGuire/MGwire,
  Merry 22, 28, 29, 58,
  63, 70, 72, 77
McGuire/MGwire (Lt) 58,
  63, 70, 77
McHaffey, Oliver 13
McIver (Daniel, Danl.)
  2, 3
McKinney, Roger 21
McKoy, Edward 15
  Malachi 24
McLean, _____ 4
  H. 3
McMahen/McMehen, John 23
McNeil, Charles 10
Mcpherson, Duncan 18
McQueen, Alexander 51
Meaddows (Jacob, Jaob) 20
Medcalf, Thomas 9
Meigler, Nicholas 27
MGuire, M. 54
Millar/Miller, John 17
Miller (Abraham, Abrahm.)
  26
  Adam 57, 60, 64-66, 68,
  71, 73
  Jacob 25
Milligan, Jacob 35
  Jno. 35
Milling (Capt) 58
  (Lt Capt) 63
Mills, Jos. 17
Moates/Motes, James 24
Moody, Rodk. 3
Moore, Isiah 27
  Morris 21
  Philip 15
Morgan, _____ 4
  Michael 26
Morning, John 22
Morris (Thomas, Thos.) 17
  (William, Wm.) 21
Morrow, Mathew 16
Moultrie (Gen) 6, 51, 59,
  66
  (Miss) 59
  Thomas 43

Moultrie/Moultry (Capt) 42
  43, 46, 48-50
Muherin/Mulherin (Charles,
  Chas.) 17
Mulcaster, John 24
Myers, Geo. 19
  Jacob 27
  Myrack, Wm. 54, 58, 63,
  70, 72, 77
Myrick (William, Wm.) 27
Myrtle, David 20

-N-

Nash, Mikel 11
Neal, Lewis 26
Nelson, John 73
Newsom (Lt) 6
Newton, _____ 46
Neyle, Phil 36
Niaurd, Thomas 23
Nipper, James 20
Norman, _____ 2
  Wm. 3, 4
Norwood, Daniel 14
  Richd. 19
  Theophilus 25
Notcher (Will., Wm.) 19
Notts (Nathaniel,
  Nathanel) 20

-O-

Oakes (James, Jas.) 3, 4
Oats (Sarg) 73
Ogier, _____ 47, 48, 50,
  53
  (Lt) 46, 49, 61, 62,
  74, 76
  George 43
Ohara/O'Harra, David 26
Oliver, Jas. 3
  Saml. 16
  (Thos., Tom.) 62, 74
O'Neal, James 3
  John 22
Orr (Dr) 36
Owens, Caleb 22
  John 18

-P-

Parham (Lt) 33
Parish, John 27
Parker, _____ 4
  (Jonathan, Jonn.) 23
Parkerson, Agnus 79
Partridge (William, Wm.)
  27, 58, 63, 70, 72,
  77
Paterson (Gen) 55
Paul, Mathew 21
  William 24
Paybody, Benjamin 17
Pearce, John 16
  Philip 17
Pennington, John 18
Peoples, Wm. 18
Perkins, Dempsey 24

Perkins (cont)
 Jesse 24
 Willis 24
Perkins/Purkins, Atheal 18
Peterkin (John, Jno.) 17,
 54, 58, 63, 70, 72,
 77
Peters, Solomon 26
Petrie,_____ 53
 (Lt) 33, 71, 73
 Alexr. 43
 (George, Geo.) 57, 60,
 64, 65, 66, 68, 69
Petty, Edwd. 18
Pickring, F. 3
Pinckney (Col) 38
 (Maj) 37, 38
 C. C. 38, 57, 60, 64,
 68, 71, 73
 Charles 36
 Charles C. 65
 Charles Cotesworth 10,
 30, 36, 37, 39, 59
 Eliza (Lucas) 36
 Thomas 9, 10, 36
Pollard (Capt) 33, 34, 58,
 63, 77
 (Lt) 11-13, 32
 (Richd., Rd.) 54, 70, 72
Pool/Pooll, Anthony 27
Porter, Uriah 27
Powell, Michael 25
 Reuben 26
Powers, Nicholas 27
Prescot (Benjamin, Benj.)
 24
 John 24
Price, John 25
 Thomas 25
Proveaux, Adrien 43
Proveaux/Provaux/Proveau/
 Preveaux (Capt) 42, 46-
 48, 50, 53, 61, 62,
 74-76
Pullam (William, Wm.) 14

-Q-

Quail, Charles 17
Quarles (James, Jas.) 27
Quarles/Quarels, Samuel 27

-R-

Ragsden, John 16
Rardall, George 9
Rasher, Peter 24
Ratliff/Ratliffe, Samuel
 23
Read, James 15
 John 24
 Robert 24
Reeves, Benj. 3, 4
Rhodes, Joseph 18
Richardson, Owen 21
Richson,_____ 4
Rife, Conrod 24
Ritchie, Robert 26
Roberts (Sarg) 75
 Jno. 4
 Joseph 69, 73
 Josh. 57

Roberts (cont)
 R. B. 7
Robertson/Robinson,
 Lamuel 27
Robison (Lt) 6
 (James, Jas.) 25
Rodemeyer/Rodemyer,
 Nicholas 22
Rogers (Lt) 46
 Ahas 18
Rollison, Gilbert 27
Rose, Cornelius 19
Roth (Lt) 78
Rotten/Routten, Robert
 27
Roux,_____ 53
 (Capt) 42, 43, 50
 Albert 43
Roy, Joseph 16
Russ, Samuel 26
Russell (William, Wm.)
 57, 60, 64-66, 68,
 71
Rutherford (Gen) 9
Rynolds, Jihua 21

-S-

Sadler, John 19
Salters, Jacob 20
Sanders, William 27
Savage, Henry 3
Sawyer,_____ 61
Scott (Col) 36, 39
 (Lt Col) 36, 38
 (George, Geo.) 19
 James 18
 John 23
 (William, Wm.) 21
Segoud,_____ 78
Sellers, Fred 16
Seward, James 24
Shannon, John 18
Shannon/Shanon, Daniel
 25
Shaw, Samuel 26
Shepherd, George 27
Shoars/Shors, Thos. 3, 4
Shubrick (Capt) 47, 50,
 56, 61, 62, 74, 75,
 76
 Thomas 43, 44
Shudy (Jhon, Jno.) 3, 4
Sibley, John 19
 William 19
Simpson (Sarg) 3
 Daniel 5
Sims, James 9
 Wm. 3
Singleton (Ambrose,
 Ambrous) 24
 James 24
Skean/Skeen (William,
 Wm.) 20
Skirving (Capt) 33
 (Lt) 10
Slater, William 21
Slicker, William 21
Smith,_____ 29
 (Capt) 58, 63, 77
 (Lt) 34, 58, 63, 70,
 77
 A. 54
 (Aaron, Arin) 19, 70,
 72

Smith (cont)
 Adam 22
 (Andrew, Andw.) 57, 60,
 64-66, 68, 71, 73
 Esau 17
 Fredk. 4
 Henry 27
 James 20, 21
 J. C. 54
 (Jesse, Jessey) 20
 John 8, 19, 24, 27
 (John C., Jno. C.) 17,
 28, 30, 63, 70, 72
 (Robert, Robt) (Rev)
 67, 68
 (Thomas, Thos.) 3, 26
Sotherland/Sutherland,
 Thomas 26
Sparrow,_____ 61, 76
 Jno. 62, 74
Spencer, Joseph 20
Springer,_____ 46, 53
 (Silvester, Silv., Syl.)
 43, 46, 47
Staple,_____ 4
Steale,_____ 2
Steel, John 18
Steele, Charles 15
 Jno. 3
Steward, John 21
Stewart,_____ 12
 Hardy 20
 William 15
Stinevender/Stinvinder,
 Cotleip 21
Stow, Joel 16
Strecham, Stepn. 3, 4
Stuart, Alexr. 3, 4
 James 6
Summerford, Jacob 20
Sutton (Samuel, Saml.) 16
Swall,_____ 4
Sweatt, James 20
Sword/Swords (James, Jas.)
 58, 63, 70, 72, 77

-T-

Tann, John 19
Tapper, Wm. 3, 4
Taylor,_____ 4
 (Capt) 13, 32
 Aaron 21
 Thomas 18
 Wm. 18
Teaster,_____ 73
 Benjn. 69
Temples, Jacob 16
 Peter 15
Theus,_____ 53
 (Capt) 10, 33, 71, 73
 (Dr) 46
 (Jeremiah, Jerh., Jh.)
 (Dr) 43, 47, 49
 Simeon 57, 60, 64, 65,
 68, 69
 Thomas, Demsey 16
 Rowland 3
Thompson (Col) 38
Thomson, Benjamin 27
Thomson (William, Wm.)
 26, 28, 29
Thring, Bunker 11
Tinsley, James 18
Towles (Capt) 6

85

Towles (cont)
  Oliver 22, 23, 28, 30
True, Thos. 18
Tucker, John 21
Turner (Capt) 10, 34
  G. 66, 71, 73
  (George, Geo.) 55, 57,
    60, 64, 65, 68, 69

-U-

Upgreve/Upgrove, Peter
  2, 3
Upgrove, Archd. 3, 4
Upshaw, William 15

-V-

Vanderhorst (Capt) 10
  (Maj) 46
  John 11, 43
Vaughan, Isaac 14, 29
Veach, Isaac 20

-W-

Wailes, _____ 4
Ward (Lt) 33
  Frederick 14
  John P. 60, 64, 68, 69
  John Peter 57, 65
  J. P. 66, 71 73
  (Richard, Richd.) 19,
    26
  W. 71, 73
  (William, Wm.) 33, 57,
    60, 64-66, 68, 69
Warley, _____ 3
  (Capt) 11, 12, 32, 33,
    47, 48, 50, 53, 61,
    62, 74-76
  F. 54, 58, 63, 72, 77
  Felix 14, 15, 28-30,
    54, 70
  G. 34, 69
  (George, Geo.) 13, 43,
    44
  J. 54
  (Joseph, Jo., Jos.) 18,
    19, 28-30, 34, 58,
    63, 70, 72, 77
Warner (Mr) 67, 68
Watson, Jacob 18
Weaver, Jacob 21
Webster, _____ 4
Wells, Edward 15
Whaley/Whaly, John 14
Wharton, Bartley 25
Whedon, James 22
Whitaker, Jno. 3
White (James, Jas.) 16,
    54, 70
  John 17
  Jonathan 18
Whitset/Whitsett, Jno.
    3, 4
Whittenton, Owen 25
Whittington (Edward, Ed.)
    20

Whittington (cont)
  Ephram 20
  Jarrod 21
Wicham, Thos. 16
Wilkins, _____ 4
Williams, _____ 4
  Jos. 63, 70, 72, 77
  Rolin 11
Williamson (Capt) 33
  Edward 26
Willson, James 20
  Robt. 18
Wilson, Ezekiel 15
  Henry 24
  James 70
  Moses 24
Windsor, Joseph 15
  (Samuel, Saml.) 26
Winn/Wynn, John 25
Wise (Maj) 9
  Samuel 28, 29
Wittenton, Burrel 19
  Isaac 19
Wmson., Isaac 3
Wood/Woods, Thomas 26
Woodford/Wodford,
  William 25
Wright (Will., Wm.) 18

-Y-

Yancy, Joseph 23
Yearly, Richd. 3
Young, William 27

www.ingramcontent.com/pod-product-compliance
Lightning Source LLC
Chambersburg PA
CBHW051948160426
43198CB00013B/2348